'TWILL BE ALL RIGHT
COME MORNIN', LUV

'TWILL BE ALL RIGHT COME MORNIN', LUV

By
Irene Hope-Hedrick

Hardback ISBN 978-1-105843-938
Paperback ISBN: 978-1-105843-945

Table of Contents

FOREWORD

Many thanks to my editor, Daniel Raymond Hedrick, my grandson who built my first computer and taught me how to use it to write my first book, *Memories of a Big Sky British War Bride* published by Globe Pequot in 2005 when I was 85 years old.

I am now looking forward to my ninety-second birthday having completed this second book which tells a tale of how a mother of four highly spirited daughters became an impassive stoic during the 20's and 30's depression days.

Thanks also to my grandson Spencer Reid Clautice Hedrick, a college student who cheers me up by fixing the Big Mac when my short term memory forgets what a download is.

Blessings to Ann Staley... Educator, essayist, poet.

Peg Elliot Mayo, psychiatric social worker, Celtic stories and readings

++++++++++++++

And a huge thank you is due to the many friends and relatives who have cheered me on to write book No. 3... Teri, Elizabeth, Ingrid, Marion, Roberta, Bibi, Stephie, John and Adeline, and old-time members of Simon Johnson's Friday Morning Writing Class.

INTRODUCTION

I happened to be an inquisitive child with a huge imagination, and whenever Mother thought I was stretching truth with fantasy, she would chastise me with the words, "That's just an old wives' tale, and nobody will believe you."

You have probably heard the phrase old wives' tales many times, and it casts aspersions that the story being told bears no truth but is merely invalid information dreamed up by women who had been denied an education themselves. They bolstered up their own lack of learning by passing along second-hand bits of information their children had brought home from school and sharing their interpretation of it with the neighbors over the garden fence.

Fortunately as time elapsed, those old wives became brave enough to step out in the open and fight for equality between the sexes. To be worthy of the same rights and privileges granted to their husbands and sons in the words signified by the forefathers of our country.

At the same time, knocking into a cocked hat the wisdom of that contrary old codger from literature Mr. Dooley says "What does a woman want iv rights whin she has priv'leges?" in Finley Peter Dunne's chapter "Rights and Privileges of Women."

Perhaps, all in good time, old wives' tales will not be thought of as balderdash but as they are intended in this book, per se, honest-to-goodness stories of a life spurred on by an aristocratically stoic mother named Emily Knight-Hope who purposely became impassible, outwardly unmoved by almost impossible situations brought about by having to raise four high-spirited daughters during the 1920s and '30s when Britain's never-ending strikes caused disastrous unemployment, leaving Father forever underfoot practicing on his tenor horn and Mother's kitchen cupboard consequently and consistently barren as Mother Hubbard's.

Father's glorious tenor voice lulled me to sleep many times to fill my hunger tantrums, and when I would sleepwalk down to those empty kitchen shelves, he would quietly tiptoe after me singing the old Irish ditty "I'll Take You Home Again Kathleen." I would enter the real world again in a flash with a haughty retort, "I am not Kathleen, Father. I am Irene!"

I dedicate this book to you, Mother, because it was not until you died that I fully understood why I never believed you loved me. It is only by writing this second volume of my memories that I realize what held our family together. There were no outward demonstrations of kissing or hugging between us. Love was demonstrated by the respect we had for one another and for the privilege of bearing the name Hope.

I loved you then, Mother, but was afraid to tell you, not knowing nor understanding you were purposely showing neither pleasure nor pain but a stoic impassiveness contrary to your real feelings. That must have been a very difficult role to play on Shakespeare's stage, but, Mother, I knew that you were not acting when you consoled your four daughters with those beloved words, "'Twill be all right come mornin', luv'" should any one of us come crying to you.

That message of hope has lived with me, has slept and wakened with me over many moons.

The philosopher Hubbard once said, "Optimism is a kind of heart stimulus—the digitalis of failure." And we simply learned from your comforting words, Mother, that there were no flies in that kind of ointment, and by the time tomorrow came, your only words of love had lulled us to sleep and to waken ready to take on a brand-new day.

CHAPTER I

THE HOPE FAMILY

The Hope family lived at No. 3 Gatewarth Street in a suburb called Sankey Bridges, skirting Warrington, an industrial town in Lancashire, northern England. I was the second of four daughters born to Harold Henry Haydn Hope and Emily Knight in our cozy cottage, each one of us in our own time. I came into the world in 1920. Today I am looking forward to celebrating my ninety-second birthday in a few months.

Father was put on this earth to love and be loved. Mother Emily (née Knight) came down from above to sit beside him and see that he did and was. Together, through thick and thin, especially during the strike-stricken years, they raised their four daughters. Our family could almost claim to be a Scottish clan, since Mother taught us to say the word "our" whenever we spoke to each other or spoke about ourselves to outsiders. For whatever reason, I always felt a wonderful sense of comfortably belonging to a family who were respectful of one another.

Eva, Irene, Joyce, and Doris were the first names chosen by Mother as each child was born in turn on her mahogany four-poster bed in the upstairs front room. Father, in due time, gave each of his children a nickname.

Eva became "our Eve" since she was the earliest one to arrive.

Doris was the smallest and youngest, and because Father had read Dickens inside and out, he nicknamed her "our little Dot."

When Joyce's time came around, he had almost cried when he came into our bedroom and said, "It's another girl!" Henceforth she bore the moniker of a boy and became "our Ike."

I was the last to hear what Irene was to become, since Father had named me Irena after the goddess of peace and hope and told me that her name should never be used in such manner as a nickname. It didn't take my sisters long to call me "our I."

Of course, Father was the only one allowed to call Mother "our Em."

Our father I remember as a scholar and a gentleman, sometimes as merry as Father Christmas himself, and someone who shared other peoples' misfortunes along with his own.

His father, Henry Charles, was a composer of music who had given each of his four sons a middle name of some famous composer. Father became Harold Henry Haydn Hope and followed in his father's footsteps, loving music and sharing his talents in every sense of the word.

Grandfather Hope was always a mystery to me. In those days long ago, I never dreamed I would be allowed to ask Grandmother any nosy questions.

The only thing voluntarily shared by Granny that remains in my long-term memory is that grandfather was an adopted baby by a very wealthy family who could afford for him to receive the best education available in the British Isles.

Sad to say, when Grandfather was in the midst of his higher education years, he was proselytized into a new church and was thereby disinherited by the Hope family. They sent him to Canada with a tutor who stayed just a short time and then absconded with Grandfather's education fund.

How and when Henry Charles returned home is still a mystery to me, because children in those days were not accustomed to asking questions of grown-ups.

Proof positive that he did return to the place of his birth in England is that he married Mary Elizabeth who bore six children named Pierce, Reginald, Harold, Beresford, Rebecca, and Mae.

When Grandfather died, Grandmother was forced to find employment and farmed out the children to live with relatives. Since there weren't enough to go around, Harold Henry Haydn Hope was assigned to an orphanage called the Bluecoat School.

When Father was telling us of the facts and fallacies he encountered at the institution, Mother, you seemed to turn a deaf ear, and I would feel sad as you left the chair empty next to mine around the fire and made your escape to another part of the house.

My heart would almost burst as Father remembered the times he would knot his bed sheets into a rope and climb through his window on the upper floor, daring to slide down this escape hatch. "But they would always chase after me, and I would get a beating for running away, the rough leather belt strikes mounting up time after time."

I have no claim to being a philosopher, but in the process of living and learning over ninety-one years, a survivor of life's ups and downs, I intend to become a centenarian to fulfill Father's promise that if I grew up with a kind heart and a sense of humor I could probably live to reach that goal.

And if you are still hearing me, Mother, nothing whatsoever in my long life has helped me bear consequences gracefully and look forward to every new tomorrow more than those blessed words you would whisper while I sat on your knee, "'Twill be all right come mornin', luv."

You lived by your own strong-willed acceptance of the here and now, Mother. I shall never forget how you turned a deaf ear, oblivious to Father's wisdom, but you would shake your head side to side as you heard him tell us about the Greeks' philosophy, "Know thyself and nothing in excess." But when you heard Goethe, the German author's comeback, "If I did know myself, I would run away," there would be a twinkle in your eye.

Actually both of those smart remarks held a whiff of hot air full of braggadocio, Mother.

Long ago William Blake wrote these words, Mother, and Father said I must think on them and soak in their wisdom if I sought to really love the life I was given.

To see the world in a grain of sand
and heaven in a wild flower
hold Infinity
in the
palm of your hand,
And Eternity
in an hour.

William Blake's words say there is a deadline to meet when eternity sits in the palm of the hand. Eternity demands, and it is relentless. It claws at the fingers impatiently leaving an itch that will never go away.

On the other hand, infinity allows us space to find joy and lasting love without fear of losing time and space and what some would call our fate.

The thorns can prick a finger; the daisies die on the chain. But season after season, the flowers, the trees, the birds, and the bees will be there in all of their glory to hold, if not in the palm of the hand, then as our eyes behold the mystery of rebirth. I have great belief in that vision of the good life open to us in the here and now, as it has lived on through the years.

You must remember that Christmas Eve in 1930, Mother! I was ten years old and in Form IV at Evelyn Street Girls' School in Warrington. My goodness, that was eighty-one years ago. Maybe I should remind you.

You had taken me to the school "do" as we called it. Father didn't want to pass his cough around the classroom, so you had no other option but to accompany me.

We arrive, my heart pounding with excitement and expectation. I am sitting at my regular desk at the back of the room, longing at that moment to be on the front row by the Christmas gifts, mostly second-hand woolen scarves and gloves donated by our own loving teachers who would never marry and have children of their own while still teaching, because mandatory single status was expected of teachers in that era. The reason was that married teachers would not be able to give full attention to schoolchildren while taking care of their own children at home.

Other gifts besides the clothing are a few white elephants donated to the cause.

Our teacher is placing all the gifts onto a low table in front of the students' desks so that, one by one, we hear our names called to choose just one object each as a Christmas present. All of them unwrapped so we might see which one we prefer. Unfortunately my seat is in the back row, and my one-and-only choice is likely to disappear all too soon. But I'm the luckiest girl in the world, Mother, and I remember you taking my hand as we trudged the long way home, the other hand snugly keeping warm the present I knew Father would dearly love.

Your first comment to Father was, "I don't know why on earth she chose something so ridiculous as a tiny china lamb, which will be broken before Christmas even gets here."

Father jumps to his feet and takes the lamb from my outstretched hand, almost shouting, "William Blake!" And he goes on, "Remember me reading to you that poem 'Little lamb who made thee, dost thou know who made thee?' And you tried to say it along with me. You would say with your eyes closed tight: 'Icke yam, icke yam, icke yam.' It was hard for you to say the letter 'l.' Well, the writer of that verse was a man of great wisdom, and you will learn much from him as you grow older."

Mother, you chose a cozy place by the fire, and that piece of china reposing on our kitchen mantelpiece seemed to draw everyone's immediate attention, relative or stranger, and I was so proud that it belonged to me.

Eventually I learned to use my tongue to pronounce the letter "l." I get a warm, happy feeling even now, Mother, remembering the way you carefully wiped away the dust from my keepsake and the nod of satisfaction you allowed yourself when you knew I would be watching.

I got over the embarrassment my sister would cause me by mimicking my tongue- tied first attempt at Blake's "Little Lamb," because Father's advice was, "If you can laugh along with those whose finger is pointing at yourself, it will bring consolation that your tormentors have failed in their attempt to ridicule and embarrass you. And, remember, when pointing his finger at you, he is pointing the rest of his fingers at himself."

Revelry in Heaven seeing the world in a grain of sand as the ocean surges to the shore where I stand and watch as the waves lick up the shore between my toes, and the ebb tide carries me along with the philosopher's words to see the world in a grain of sand.

There has been revelry in heaven making chains of the daisies, ready to pick them again as they rise with their season. I have walked the countryside in my childhood, discovering enough species of wildflowers to fill three large-size drawing books with those lovely flowers, pressed and labeled with their common and scientific family names, their habitation, and any other pertinent information I could find in my research.

Mother, you never praised me for that accomplishment in the year 1930, but then I had been negligent of expressing my thanks to you for preserving and watching over them until my visit back home in 1948 when you confessed, "I finally had to throw them out, luv. They were getting moldy."

Eva was in secondary school and was begging me to let her take the flower books to show her classmates—remember, Mother?—and I agreed. Well, she was requested to enter them in the secondary school science project, and the books won the first and only prize. Eva had raced home with two leather-bound volumes titled *Wayside* and *Woodland Blossoms,* with 394 beautifully illustrated species by Edward Step. Our Eve assumed she could keep those precious books, but you, dear Mother, lost no time taking them from her hands and placing them in mine with just a frown and a smile. How I wanted to hug you at that moment, Mother.

Heaven in a wildflower! Joy! Beautiful things of repeating glory we can hold in the palm of a hand. Infinity.

There is no touch or feeling in the meaning of that word, but it is the here and now while eternity snaps its fingers to bring each one of us down to earth and under.

I was taught to learn and remember. To trust and forgive. To find joy and lasting love without fear of losing time and space and what some would call our fate. The rose can prick our fingers. The daisies die on the chain. But season after season, they will be there in all of their glory to hold in the palm of my hand.

I find infinity following the bold brushstrokes of Joseph Mallard Turner's masterpiece of a landscape with a river. I follow it to the vanishing point in his creation, where lies the unquestionable promise of hidden beauty beyond, knowing there will always be another season to gather wild roses along a country road. To watch a beautiful butterfly emerge and take wing from a chrysalis that was once a caterpillar. And I find joy in life's abundance and revel in its promise.

I walk around the pond on the way from school and see a mound of jelly spotted with small black blobs of something. I cup my hands to scoop it up and take it home in my empty lunch bucket.

I watch the miracle of life as those little black things, protected in their bed of spawn floating on top of a kitchen bowl, transform into the shape of a head and a body.

Racing home from school to watch this miracle of metamorphism enacted, I see a tail and four legs appearing sporadically here and there until they are able to wriggle free from their nest and learn to swim. At that point, Mother, you insisted I throw them back into the pond to fend for themselves.

Well, racing ahead at this moment to the year 2011, here I am watching another miracle of nature I must share, Mother.

In a stupor of bereavement last Saturday, my armchair quarterback and I were actually moaning the presumed loss of an O.S.U. football game.

Yes, he is an English friend who loves watching football on my big screen while his wife stays home tending her beautiful flower garden and making tomato sauce out of a few leftover tomatoes from their vegetable "community sharing" patch.

I tried to up the spirit of the day and opened a box of Amy's Spinach Pizzas, and they cheered up the situation along with a cup of tea.

But sometimes my mind needs to wander away from a disappointing show, and I glanced over at the bay window to see if the large spider was still looking through it after goggling at me for a whole week and never moving.

Well, somebody had been at work out there on the big window. My spider had spun a beautiful web all around him, with a delicate silk thread leading way up to anchor on to the right-hand corner and a similar thread down to the left corner of the windowpane. And some people don't think wild life creatures can think for themselves, Mother?

Ron took a quick look to see what I was puzzling over and said, "He's a big one. He's been overeating."

I said, "I haven't seen him leave the center of his web, and I was wondering what I could give him to eat, since he seems nailed to that beautiful home he created."

"Just wait a second, and you'll see him move. See the fly on that silk tight rope to you right? Watch what happens to him and you'll be amazed!"

Well, I couldn't believe my eyes. The spider was mincing his way along the delicate strand to reach his dinner, which I expected him to gobble up without asking permission. But no, in some mysterious way, he actually spun a cocoon around the fly, hung him by a string, and hauled him to his resting place in the center of the web. Slowly the cocoon rose up to meet his fate.

"Watch this now," Ron said. I was puzzled as I watched the carcass of the fly drop from the spider's hold.

"Didn't the spider like the taste of him?" I ask.

Ron just grinned and said, "Well, he doesn't exactly eat his prey. He just sucks the juice out of them and let's them go."

I had to share that miracle of nature with you, Mother, before my short-term memory lets go. I shall be ninety-two on the fourth of May. Remember that day in 1920? You would be surprised to learn, I have a dream occasionally that takes me precariously through the intricacies of birthing. And the doctor's found, through a CAT scan after a fall, that I have the brain of a very young woman. Did you know that, Mother?

Putting religious beliefs on hold and ruminating the heavy burden of eternity in your hand, even for an hour, chewing on the dismal ruminations of where and how this world may end, puts a damper on the beauty we see before our eyes morning, noon, and night. You can live a good, happy life if it is free from illusion.

To be who you are rather than whom you would prefer to be!

"Que Sera, Sera! Whatever Will Be, Will Be!"

Those simple rules have taken me through ninety-one years of loving and learning.

That does not simply mean we should expect and accept everything that happens through life uncaringly. For we are blessed with feelings both of joy and of sorrow and each is dependent on the other.

The rainbows of joy could never brighten the heart if the arrows of sorrow had not first pierced the soul to bear the burden.

Whatever will be, will be ... the sweet and the sour, the rough and the smooth, the joy and the sorrow. It has all been there throughout my long life, spurred along by my father's words forever reminding me, "If you grow up with a kind heart and a sense of humor, luv, you'll live to be a hundred."

That seemed like eternity when I was only seven and worried what I would look like when I became a grown-up, Mother.

I had a taste of what it could be like to be old and useless from my Father when I was seven or eight years old.

Mother, you didn't even look up to welcome him as you were brushing your beautiful, long, black hair of which you were very proud. I always wondered why you didn't think it was so beautiful by plaiting it into a pigtail and winding it into a bun at the back of your neck.

Yet it was, as the old brush strokes revealed so very beautiful that night. So boldly beautiful in the ugly room. The soft blue lights of Christmas danced along each strand as the comb caressed the black, black length of it, a raven's wing touching your shoulders. I could hear the clean squeak as your fingers parted the tresses, twisting and lifting them until everything lovely was eaten up and scraped into a tight, black knot at the back of our head. It was neater that way, you said. There were a few straggling tendrils that loved freedom too much, and I laughed with them as they sprang away from your red, rough hands.

I stared at all of my secret places, looking for beauty in that ugly room. But that night, even the flowers on the wallpaper stared back at me, pale and lifeless, when I tried to breathe life into their dead flat petals and touch their velvet to my cheek.

I hated them because they had been beautiful, but now they were dead, and I locked them up with the blue lights in your black hair, Mother.

I longed for beauty. I sought it in the scrubbed and polished floor that sang of marbled halls and crinolines, of twinkling buckles and dancing feet. Red satin and blue velvet of my dream fabric swirled and faded in the tight, black knot that was your hair. Just that afternoon you had scrubbed the old, red floor tile until it shone, preparing for a special guest who dropped in on most people this time of year. Some said he came in down the chimney, but I could never imagine anyone as beautiful as Saint Nicholas covered with soot. Some said he came only to good children, but I thought that wasn't fair, because I always remembered that part too late. I was too big to cry, they said.

Before I could ask what Father Christmas would bring that year, my father's strong arms were lifting me up to his shoulders, and I was a giant walking through the doorway into the cold December night. He pointed to a star in the sky, a star as bright as the light in his eyes, and when he spoke, there were falling leaves rustling among his words. I caught them as they fell. "Let me tell you a story, luv," he said.

The words of his story whispered of three men who followed the star. Rich men they were, riding camels through the sand, camels with saddlebags holding gifts for a king. I wondered what frankincense and myrrh were, but who could ask such a question when beauty was in the air? My father's voice robbed the saddlebags and gave those gifts to me, and I placed them, gently, among the blue lights in the braided black hair.

We might have gone back through the doorway then, back to the ugly room, but we didn't. Father walked toward the cottage next door, and I became afraid, for in the dark, ghosts and dead men lurked in the tall grass over there, and they'd made tut-tutting noises at me once because they didn't know what children were. Virginia creeper bearded the face of the house, and shiny eyes of windows blinked at our intrusion. I held tight as he ducked low in the doorway and went inside.

The old couple sat huddled at the hearth, as if, like the dying bit of fire, they, too, had almost gone out. They seemed not even to have the will to lift the poker and shake down the ashes from the glowing coals, and I knew the meaning of a word I had never heard. Despair was all around me.

It was heavy in my hands as they slid down from my father's neck. It was heavy in my feet as they touched the cold floor. Hunger and pain and emptiness stared at me from their cold, pale eyes, and the wrinkles in their faces did not make a smile around their lips. I became an old, old woman as I sat with them by the fire.

"Merry Christmas," my father said, and they never looked up at him as they said the same.

Silently, gray ashes fell from the grate as the last wisp of smoke coiled slowly up the chimney, the smell of death riding its back. Still, the smile in my father's eyes would have paled the star, and his gentle "Merry Christmas" spoke to me the secret of life. I understood, in that moment, that charity can be given with an empty hand, and I felt wiser than the wise men.

Oh, what gifts I could have given. Gold. The frankincense. The myrrh. Blue velvet and my mother's hair. If only I could make them smile! My heart was bursting with loving and giving, yet I had nothing but myself to give. My gifts were all locked up in my mother's hair.

I wanted to strip the flowers from the wall, petal by petal, without bruising their loveliness. I wanted to shake those frail old people and make them glad to be alive. I wanted them to leap up and dance with me until all the bubbles burst. But they didn't know how to see!

I could have turned them around three times and pointed them to the mystery that would open their eyes. But children don't teach games to grownups.

The star still shone on high, lighting our way back to the ugly room, and I became a little girl again, wanting a doll for Christmas. A doll with pretty blue lights in her long, black hair. And eyes that opened and shut.

And so it has been throughout my life. A search for beauty. A longing after truth.

The cold, fish-blue eyes of that old man and woman, staring so fixedly into the dying embers of their life together, gave a seven-year-old child a grim picture of what the far distant future could look like when she became old and ready to die.

I looked into my father's eyes, which were hazel like mine, for before that cold day, I had thought he, too, was old, as most children believe of people taller than themselves. But no, his eyes were young and alive, alight with another kind of flame that would never flicker and die. Alive with a mystical knowledge of truth and love that gently shone from their depths.

I determined that I, too, should have eyes like my father's, even if mine grew dim and could no longer see the beauty that I sought.

"Is life worth living?"

"This is a question for an embryo, not for a man," replies Samuel Butler.

Ask that question to this old woman, and I can vouch for every living second, except a few short-term memory lapses, to be richly rewarding in many ways. And at this very moment, your words, Mother, "'Twill be all right come mornin', luv," are keeping me awake with hope and longing to hear them again, alive to pave my way for tomorrow.

MOTHER'S THIRD EYE

Another reminder of you, dear Mother, is coming into focus before my very eyes, even though they grow dimmer and my fingers more crooked as I stretch another day into a possible one hundred years of using them wisely as you always did. Remember? You never gave up, and you never doubted you would be there for us even when we were old enough to care for ourselves. As Blake once said, "If the sun and moon should ever doubt, they would go out!" Your star will live on forever, Mother.

My sisters and I always had an inkling that you were blessed with a third eye hidden in the back of your head by your beautiful, black hair. In fact we decided it was magical; otherwise, how on earth could you have been so sure that "everything would be all right come morning, love?"

To me those precious words were God's own truth sent by virtue of Mother's third eye and convincing me to believe there was always a new day coming to look forward to, whether it bring hail, rain, or pain. Proof that whatever the weather, the clouds will soon dry up and die.

Proof positive of Mother's blessing was given to me when I was in the third form at Evelyn Street Girls' School—old enough to hold back my tears and my fears.

Early one cold wintry morning, I stood by the fireguard, the wire and brass contraption that kept us from getting too close to the hot coals and sparks they sometimes crackled out. I was hanging on tightly to the guard that morning, not because I was afraid of catching fire but because every time I opened my eyes there was nothing there. "Ma'am," I was screaming at the top of my voice. "I can't see! There's nothing there. Everything's gone black."

Mother was there in a flash, gently prying my fingers from the fireguard and moving me backwards until I felt the edge of the rocking chair as she sat me down in it.

"Now then. You just sit there and don't worry. Don't move, and I'll make you a nice 'ot cuppa tay and a spot o' Granny's ginger wine. You'll be right as rain by the time you start for school. You'll see."

And I believed her! Maybe she had read the tealeaves in my cup again, and maybe she was asking God if he would care to help, and he had given her a quicker answer than he ever seemed to give me when I asked for anything. But I believed with all my heart that "everything's going to be all right now, luv."

In the few minutes it took to drink my cuppa, Mother had managed to bring my eyesight back to where it belonged. A teaspoonful of ginger wine down my throat to stave off that cold wind, and I was on my way to feeling better when I got there.

Father had given this family eye of Mother's the name faith ever since our little Dot was run over on the Main Road. She was only six years old and had been crossing the highway safely on her way to school for several months when the accident happened.

Mother's timeless caution to the four of us had always been, "Stay together now, and don't be late." But Doris had lagged behind without our noticing, and we were way ahead of her on that fateful day when she was left standing on the sidewalk, afraid to cross that road without our help to watch out for the empty spaces between the dangerous fast vehicles racing from Manchester to Liverpool.

On that school day long ago, while our little Dot was standing on the side of the road, a lorry carrying a big heavy load had swung around the bend at full speed where she was standing and sideswiped our little Dot, leaving her unconscious on the sidewalk.

The first Mother heard of this was from an onlooker who ran the several blocks from the madding crowd to our house and screamed from the front door, "Emily, your little Dot! She's been run over by a lorry. She's lying there, just lying there not moving, Emily. Flat as a pancake!"

We three older girls slept in Mother's big bed that fear-filled night while our parents were at the hospital, watching over our little sister who was still unconscious. Mother stayed there, day and night, while Father took care of us at home. We were allowed to see Doris, even though she stayed in that condition for six long weeks. I would hear Mother say, as she smoothed our Dot's hair away from her forehead, "It's going to be all right now, luv. You'll see. It's going to be all right. I'll see to that!" Mother could just plain see it with that wonderful third eye that Father called faith, and when our little Dot finally opened her eyes, she turned to Mother and said, "You're still here?" And Mother simply told her, "Yes, I'm still here, luv, and I'll be here all night, but I have to go home in the morning and do the washing."

When Mother would hang out the washing to dry in the top garden—a field of grass at the end of our street with the same dimensions as the houses alongside—she would allow us to sit on the top rung of the turnstile bordering the railway crossing so that we could watch the trains go by. And as I sit here today, an old woman computing my life, I am remembering the lines from Robert Louis Stevenson's poem "From a Railway Carriage." I would sing the rhyme along with the music coming from the wheels as the train ran the rails.

Faster than fairies, faster than witches,
Bridges and houses, hedges and ditches;
And charging along like troops in a battle
All through the meadows the horses and cattle:
…. Here is a cart runaway in the road
Lumping along with man and load;
And here is a mill, and there is a river:
Each a glimpse and gone forever!

No, Mr. Stevenson, not gone forever. Your words, their rhythm keeping pace with your intended motion, have kept me going through three children, five grandchildren, one great-grandson, and a second great-grandson expected in a few months. Such are the joys I still feel in my life. Your pufferbilly train was real, and you took me along for the ride while I sat on the stile. I'm off again now as far as I see, living a good life through infinity.

Even though we had mother's permission to sit on that stile so close to the railway tracks, the fence on the other side was forbidden territory since its whole purpose for being there was to protect little children from falling into the Stinking Brook, as mother called it.

But mother was right there with her stoic strength, saving our Eve when she fell off that fence in spite of her warning about the poisonous effluent the water carried from the White Lead Paint Company nearby, saying we'd have no one to blame but ourselves if we sat on the top railing of that fence and fell into water rushing all that muck to God only knows where.

Well, somebody actually pushed our Eve so that she fell headfirst into the Stinking Brook, sinking down into and under the water as it carried her along, surging toward the tunnel ready to swallow up our poor Eve forever.

Fortunately some big lads with sticks had jumped down to play near the tunnel entrance and heard us screaming as we pointed toward my sister. They dared to get their pant legs wet, with arms outstretched waiting to grab Eve's clothing and haul her to the edge of the water and up the bank just seconds away from her being swallowed up into the dark of that big black hole. As the boys helped her to slither under the bottom railing of the fence, I could see her hands at her throat as if she were choking.

Two of the lads made a seat by grasping each other's wrists with one hand and their own wrist with the other hand, and some of the other kids lifted her on to the makeshift seat. I took one look at Eve and raced home, fortunately close as the end of the street, shrieking, "Mum, Dad! Come on, quick. Our poor Eve nearly drowned, and she looks like a big, black dog."

"Oh, God! I told them to stay away from that bloody stinking brook," you said as you bolted past Father like the wind and reached the garden gate to see Eva slumped between the two boys. "She's not breathing!" you had muttered, Mother, holding back your own breath in fear. "Get her inside and lift her up on to the kitchen table 'arold," you ordered Father.

There was nothing at hand that resembled a life-saving object, so Mother did what she always did. She made do with what she had and stuck her little finger into Eva's mouth to crook out whatever she felt didn't belong there. Then, tilting back poor Eve's head slightly, she opened her mouth to gently push two more fingers inside far enough to the throat to make Eva gag and throw up whatever else was lodged further down. Mother heaved a sigh, "She's breathing again. You'll be all right now, luv." She eased a spoonful of laxative into her mouth and whispered in her ear, "Try to keep that down now. Don't you fret now, luv. You'll be ready for school in the mornin'."

"'Arold, we'll need that kettle of hot water on the hob, and make me a cuppa tay while you're at it."

"Our I, go and tell those nosey parkers at the door to go home and mind their own business. Then come back and help me with this mess, and get your sister into my bed.

Counting those narrow steps up to mother's bedroom and lifting my poor sister up on to a resting place, my mind raced back to the last Christmas Eve when my sisters and I rejoiced in that very bed.

We were snuggled up on top of the eiderdown covering that big four-poster, a wedding dowry Granny Knight had insisted on mother bringing to her new household.

Eyes all aglow, ears alert, and listening for the first soft notes of Father's Penketh Tannery Prize-Winning Band!

With the window pushed up, the neighbors already on the street down below and four little girls in red flannel shimmies, hanging over the windowsill, elbows pushing space, and everyone in hearing range singing as the band played on carol after carol, until they were all played out.

Then came the hush, and father was saying words of welcome to his humble home, then watching the musicians (all of them men in those ancient times) as they traipsed into the house singing, "Good King Wenceslas looked out ..."

We dared to barge downstairs for Father's goodnight kiss and were allowed to take just one gold-wrapped coin hanging from the kissing bush before mother's expected but unwelcome words, "Off to bed with you now, like good children."

But I knew the wassailing would last until the wee hours, what with the sherry and the mince tarts and Granny's year-old, brandy-soaked Christmas pudding. So I crept quietly on my way to the other bedroom and sat on the third stair down, hoping no one would spot me there as I watched the celebration. Year after year I would do this, just to hear mother laughing and hugging as she always did on this wonderful night. And when people would pat her on the hand and say, "I've never tasted better tarts, Emily," she knew they were right.

When Uncle Harry (her eldest brother, who served his country honorably with some famous regiment in the First World War; it was either with the Scotch Terriers or the Black Watch) put his arms around her and pecked her on the cheek, saying, "Nobody bakes them like you do, Emily," I saw her pull the hanky from her pinafore pocket and turn her head away.

ONCE ON A CHRISTMAS MORNING
Christmas is coming
The goose is getting fat
Would you please to put a penny
In the old man's hat
If you haven't got a penny
A ha'penny will do
If you haven't got a ha'penny
God Bless You

My sisters and I would sing in chorus as that Holy Day came "creeping in on little cats' feet" as poet Faulkner describes the fog, and it was in nail-biting anguish that we looked in every nook and niche in our home, not finding a present hidden there.

It was Christmas morning, the night after I learned how to grow old. The depression days in the 1920s, when Father was a victim of the everlasting strikes in England and "on the dole."

Mother had been sitting in Father's rocker for days on end before that very special Christmas Eve in our little cottage on Gatewarth Street in Sankey Bridges.

Her crochet hook poking down through another hole in the sequence of stitches and pulling up yet another thread as the tiny dress took shape before my very eyes. As she finished that garment, she started a second one, until there were two of everything— dresses, booties, and bonnets—all of which she placed neatly in the kitchen bureau's bottom drawer.

I dared to ask, "Who are those for, Mother?"

"Oh, I'm just making them for someone's new baby" she said.

"Will the new baby be that small, ma'am?" I dared to ask. "Maybe ..." The tone in her voice said "that's enough questions now," and I gave the matter no more thought.

Christmas morning always came early at our house, the excitement bubbling and occasionally spilling over into tears for one reason or another, even when Father could spend a few pennies.

That particular December morning, I had awakened to find on my bed the most beautiful baby doll I had always dreamed of, a cuddly rag body with china limbs and a beautiful, smiling china face. She was wearing a crocheted pink dress and matching booties and a bonnet of the same color.

I picked up my brand-new doll, and, yes, her eyes were bluer than I ever dreamed, as the long black lashes opened and shut when I rocked her up and down.

I had never loved anything more, but in the rush to share my good fortune with the world, I ran out of the room so fast I slipped on the landing, falling head-over-heels down the stairs, bouncing against every one of those wooden steps and shattering the smiling face of my new doll.

Unable to stand my tears, our Eve, my older sister said, "Here, you can hug mine for a while, but I want it back!" I kept glancing at her to see if she was about to snatch it away, but she left it with me for a long time.

Meanwhile, Mother rubbed a little bit of butter on my bruises, and Father found a pot of glue and tried to put the pieces of my doll's head back together.

But she wasn't truly beautiful after that. Her lashes stayed glued shut and her lips no longer seemed to be smiling.

Our mother, always one for making the best of things, said, "Never you mind, luv. You can both be a mother to your sister's doll. Now hush your crying. Everything will be all right come mornin', luv. You just wait and see!"

And the love in your voice just somehow made it so, Mother.

Chapter II

GRANDMOTHER KNIGHT

La Rochefoucauld once coined the phrase: "To establish oneself in the world one does all one can to be established there already," and those words describe Granny Knight to a tee. She was born and blessed with the gift of reckoning, adding up columns of figures in her head.

In the days before sound was introduced to movies, the words in the silent pictures were written underneath the action in every flip of the screen. I saw lots of those silent pictures, many of them in the horror category, when Mother insisted I accompany Granny Knight whenever she decided to go to the pictures, so I could read the script underneath the action on the screen.

It was always a mystery to me why curiosity never got the best of Granny. She was denied any schooling so that she could stay home to help her mother raise their large family of eight. But surely her brothers and sisters could have taught her what they had learned in school, to read by herself anyway, and saved me from a lot of nightmares. I could never understand how she derived any pleasure from those horror stories, and even though I had to keep my eyes glued on the words she wanted to hear, I would dare myself to squint up at the grisly characters now and then.

The night I saw the club-footed man, I started to shiver, and it wasn't even cold. He was dressed in black, a cape hugging his shoulders and wearing a top hat, which seemed to fall off his head as he slouched down, dragging his lame foot behind and feeling his way with a silver-handled cane poking between the cobblestones.

Grandmother poked me in the arm and asked, "What's he going to do now?" I just told her I didn't know, because I hadn't read between the lines on cue.

Walking Granny home late at night was a nightmare in itself, and I was always glad to see the lamplighter walking down the street with his ten-foot pole lighting up the globe on top of the lamppost. Granny hung heavy on my arm, and her girth slowed me down considerably as I tried to hurry on past the alleyways where the cats were doing their prowling and screaming, daring me to come closer as those strangely luminous eyes betrayed them in their furtive pursuits.

Mother allowed me to stay overnight at Granny's house on "picture" nights, and I usually enjoyed it once I got there. That night, though, I asked her for a safety pin, hoping she wouldn't ask what for, and when she did, I had to tell her I wanted it to pin my nightgown to the sheets so that I wouldn't be able to get out of bed and sleepwalk, as I sometimes did, and find myself in the alley with the cats and that black-hearted villain with his silver-tipped cane. And Father would not be there to wake me up and lead me back to bed, nor you there to assure me with your words, Mother, "'Twill be all right come mornin', luv."

Grandmother tried to comfort me, yet all those horrible hours in the smoke-filled Pavilion theatre on the village green, end of the parade of shop, would not go away, even when I tried to imagine the pavilion when the silent screen had been a stage with its gold-tasseled, red velvet drop curtains and gilded box seats designed for a royal view of stars, maybe like Sir Lawrence Olivier and Helen Terry. Or a vaudeville show where Murgatroid and Winterbottom would challenge my hearing to keep up with their fast-paced witty humor. But my mind would come back to the dark, sinister alley of that silent picture long after the gas jet over the mantel had been turned off and grandmother's heavy footsteps were echoing down the hall, a chill, club-footed reminder that there would be a next time.

Even so I knew Mother would be waiting for me after school with a jam *buttie* and whispering in my ear, "Did Grandmother thank you for your reading the pictures to her, luv? There aren't many your age who could read like that you know. You're a clever girl, our I."

Grandfather Knight was a sea captain who sailed the world around between short visits with his family, counting up to eight at home before he died.

GRANDMOTHER MARY ELIZABETH HOPE TRIFLING WITH TRUFFLES

Serious things cannot be understood at all without laughter things, nor opposites at all without opposites.
—Plato

There was nothing really trifling about Granny Hope, nicknamed Polly for her years of housekeeping for such notable people as Sir John Moores and his family and old time British actors Tom Walls and Ralph Lynn who loved her brand of tea along with her spritely nature and sense of humor.

History repeats itself as a glance at old books reveals, so as a youngster, I determined I would never become wrinkled and cranky like most people I knew. So I set my mind and heart on growing up to be a replica of my father's mother, my grandmother Mary Elizabeth Hope.

She had been a widow for as long as I could remember, her husband, my grandfather Henry Charles Hope having died and left her to raise their six children without a penny in her pocket.

Father showed me some of the poetry his father had written, and poets have never been known for the wages they earn, so that is understandable.

Whoever tagged the nickname Polly on this lovely, proper English, genteel soul, whom I adored, must have been a very close acquaintance and knew her love for a good old cuppa Mazawattee tea. She would stop at our home on her long walks to town from the suburbs during the war when petrol was filling up war tanks instead of buses and other vehicles for transportation.

Sure enough, Mother would set the old blackened teakettle to sing on the hob as she chipped up a couple of potatoes for the ever-ready pan of lard.

Polly would announce her presence with the brass door knocker pounding out the same old rhythmic hi-tidelly hi-tie, POM POM, then mincing her way down the lobby and into the kitchen, singing the old nursery rhyme, "Polly Put the Kettle On."

On this special occasion, to our astonishment, Polly announced, "We'll skip the tea today, Emily. I decided that you and I should teach your girls how to make chocolate truffles. Now, give me the key to your liquor cabinet, Emily, and I'll see what kind of assortment you have that we can use, because the best truffles always need a spot of Crème de Menthe or a shot of Grand Marnier. Or Sandeman's Sherry if you have that ...

Mother drew in a quick, sharp breath and let it out slowly and purposefully retorting, "You know perfectly well, as does your son, Polly, that I have never in my whole life touched a drop!" We could all vouch for that, because even when Father stopped at the pub for a quick one when we reached the top of Hill Cliff on our Sunday walk, Mother would stay out in the garden with the lemonade and the children.

"Oh, well. Never mind! It's a good thing I brought my own," said Gran, digging into the large, black leather handbag with the shiny gold knobs on the rim that twisted the purse open and shut. Flushing out a small flask of something or other and shaking her head from side to side, she said to Mother, "It might do you good to take a spot of this now and then, Emily! Now, let's take a look in your scullery. I know you don't have an ice box in which to let the chocolate cool and set! But you might have a piece of marble somewhere in this old house."

Trying to look disappointed, Mother's chest expanded as she took in a breath of air, letting it out slowly in a sigh of relief.

"Sorry, Polly, I'm afraid the only bit of marble around here is the top of my dressing table upstairs. You'll never be able—"

"Oh, lets give it a try, Emily," Gran butted in. "All we need is a few extra hands." I could see Mother's stoic determination rising up against Polly's chagrin at being thwarted of a chance to show off her culinary expertise. For hadn't she been housekeeper for those famous film stars?

"It would be impossible," Mother said, "for two women and four skinny children to handle the man-sized job of carting something that heavy down all those narrow stairs!"

But Polly was adamant. Hadn't everything she touched in the homes of her famous employers had an aura of the aristocracy about it? And didn't Ralph Lynn and Tom Walls provide her with the best of everything to keep a good house for them? She had prepared gourmet meals for them time after time. And it would be no different making chocolates in this house, if she could help it!

"Well, well, then we'll just have to get some helping hands, won't we?"

Without a second's hesitation our Ike said, "Oh, I bet those lads outside will help us Granny." And out she shot to bring them in, while Mother sat down in Father's chair with such a wallop the chair started rocking all by itself. She mopped her forehead with her pinny, letting out a groan of defeat, and said, "Well, there you are then, Polly. You've got all the help you need, but be careful you don't bang into any of my furniture or the new paint job that 'arold's just finished. *And* you had better keep it away from the skirting boards holding up the walls, or the whole damn staircase might very well give in on you."

She said this with a quick, contemptuous sneer with her lip, and quietly said to me,

"Go put the kettle on again, luv, and you and I will just sit here and have a nice, hot cuppa tea."

With all hands on deck, the slab in question was easy to uproot from the dresser top it covered, but once free from that, there was the precarious problem of twisting and turning around corners and edging it down our narrow staircase. Eventually it was nudged into the kitchen, and only after Mother had slowly but purposely removed the brown teapot and cups from the table and folded up the newly washed white linen cloth that beautiful slab of marble was set down, not too gently, with sighs of relief.

Granny was already rolling up her sleeves and unpacking enough butter and cream to keep busy until the cows came home to make some more. I kept a sharp eye on the chocolate, but Polly's eye was quicker still and constantly on the huge bureau mirror facing the fireplace, reflecting every move I made whilst unwrapping the Cadbury's chocolate ready to add to her butter and other ingredients.

Her precise instructions continued to keep everyone in a dither, leading into mayhem, what with spills of costly ingredients from the pan spilling over onto the hob, too hot now for a dip-in with a little finger, and there was Big Tom, our fat, lazy cat just sitting there grinning at it all.

The truffle making was a huge disaster, but when Mother was mumbling words like disgraceful and wasteful as the brown, shiny mixture was poured out and spread into a large pancake on the marble, we four girls were compensated with the fruits of our labor when Polly, looking directly at Mother, said, "The girls can scoop up this Grenache into balls resembling truffles now, Emily." And picking up her brandy bottle, she smilingly waved it in the air for Mother to see, saying, "You won't be needing this now, will you, Emily?"

Mother flushed a beet-root red and didn't deign to reply as Polly put her hat back on her head, secured it with the long hatpin to her graying hair, picked up the brandy bottle once more from its temporary perch on the sideboard, and stuffed it into her big, black bag.

Lifting up her coat from the hook behind Father's newly stained door, she gave it a quick shake and slung it over her arm. The parting words I caught as she headed down the lobby. "Well, ta-ta then. We'll try again another day, shall we girls?"

Mother usually had the last word at our house, but she muttered them to herself this time, "That day will never come, Polly!"

Granny Hope caused a stir wherever she went, and a visit to her podiatrist was no exception. Along with her five senses, a little extra perception making up the sixth one, she was also endowed with a sixth toe, which necessitated painful treatments on that foot periodically. At one of those times, Polly was feeling a little delicate and swooned over in a faint in spite of clenching her teeth, along with her toenails, to suffer through the pain.

The quick-thinking podiatrist had the presence of mind to grab the bottle of brandy in his desk drawer and measured out a tot, hoping a quick sniff from the glass would revive her. It took a couple of whiffs for her to come to and realize she was due for more pain than she could tolerate, so she grabbed the glass from the doctor's hand and fortified herself, swallowing the whole tot of brandy.

The visits to her podiatrist became more frequent from that day on, and strangely enough the minute he took out his tools to work on her extra digit, she would slink down in the chair in a swoon, with one eye squinting at her old doc setting out two glasses and a half-full bottle.

Everybody loved Polly, and so did her podiatrist. He enjoyed her company and loved her wit, and I can imagine him, whenever he had occasion, raising his glass in a hearty toast to Polly's sixth toe.

I have a picture of Grandmother Hope celebrating her first century birthday, with a beautiful cake nearby and loving family and friends surrounding her bed, mulling over her longevity, the telegram of congratulations from Her Majesty the Queen of England, and even more so, a visit from actress Barbara Clegg, granddaughter of Sir John Moores whose family Polly had helped raise. My sister Joyce was invited to Barbara's wedding and mailed pictures and programs for me to see the luxurious red carpet and settings. I have often wished I could locate this famous star to thank her for visiting grandmother on her 100th birthday; "the most wonderful present I ever had," boasted Granny! She lived to be 103, almost a miracle in those long ago days.

CHAPTER III

LORD LEVERHULME

"He … met every kind of person except the ordinary person. He loved every body, so to speak, except everybody."

Chesterton wrote those words, and I attribute them to one of the most upright men I have ever seen walking this good earth since I took my first step.

Growing up, my sisters and I had little in the way of toys and entertainment, but we didn't ask for much, because we had Lord Leverhulme and his great benevolence, providing means and opportunities in life that otherwise would never be within our reach.

He was the founder of Joseph Crosfield and Sons Limited, a soap factory in Warrington, who also owned other soap factories throughout the land, eventually converging them all under the corporate name Unilever Limited, who extended their range of products to include everything from soap to soup and nuts around the world.

I had great respect for this gentleman, because he treated his employees royally, providing recreation facilities with hockey fields, tennis courts, bowling greens, and cricket grounds. A ballroom and theater were added by our benefactor, giving opportunity to employees and their families to participate in events held there.

Though Father was not employed at the factory, my sisters and I were invited to join the troupe. We rehearsed operettas and pantomimes all summer long every year in order to show the public how talented one might become with practice. During teachers' rest holiday week in the fall, we performed live.

Night after night a packed audience watched our show, at three shillings and sixpence a ticket, all of which paid for a lovely holiday at Llandudno in Wales for the company retirees.

I loved every night of that adventure-filled week, an eight-year-old wearing makeup. Remember, Mother, we walked home slowly every night, because you would scrub off the paint from our lips and cheeks the minute we got there? We were really upset about that. We weren't getting into any mischief, were we?

But we couldn't do without you those days could we now, Mother? I never dreamed of thanking you for sitting hour after hour at your old Singer treadle sewing machine, making every costume needed by the cast of Dick Whittington, Pearl of the Ocean Wave, and Cinderella to name a few? You were the pearl of every show in which I performed. And I never realized that your pride was too invincible to ask for money since your daughters were enjoying a productive and exciting childhood along with worldly experience to guide their future.

Let the show begin then!

Our Eve never lauded it over me, but she was the shining star in the Hope family. She could portray any character on stage and off, and she earned the right to be a star performer.

My big thrill, while belonging in all of the presentations, was on a high stool, my costume protected by an apron tied around my neck, an ugly duckling waiting to be transformed into a beautiful swan. Crimson lipstick and deep blue eye shadow were blended in where they belonged over a skin-colored paste that was darker than my naturally pale complexion, and in a few moments I would be facing the footlights looking alive rather than a pale, wan, ghost who might have scared away the audience.

I sat tapping my fingers with anticipation, waiting for the company orchestra to tune up their instruments into a cacophony of sound that took my breath away. Here a bassoon booming. There a fiddle floundering, cymbals clashing in between, violins reaching and caching the high notes to heaven. Muted trumpets butting in a bar or two.

Up and down the scales they rambled, the pianist accompanying them. I knew no words then to describe the ecstasy of that haunting, dissonant, musical flight of fancy, but even now, as I listen, the sounds come waltzing back.

I see myself, on stage, waiting for the overture to end and the opening bars of Dick Whittington to begin. I am there, once more, singing my heart out as the red velvet curtains part to show a full house of expectant people willing to listen.

What child could ask for more?

Our Eve and I had qualified for parts in the adult opera performances and the annual Drama Festival, which was an exciting opportunity. The company theatre was well attended and enthusiastically received, giving us hope for winning the coveted cup when we competed at the yearly Drama Festival against players from Port Sunlight and the several other Lever Brothers firms throughout the country.

Our Eve was especially delighted upon learning we would celebrate my premiere performance at the Fortune Theatre on Drury Lane in London, where the likes of Lawrence Olivier and Helen Terry took their bows before the footlights.

London was awake and awaiting as we arrived that morning so long ago, eager to see and be seen. The whole entourage of cast members, stage crew, and a couple of company executives who rode in Mr. Worthington's car were greeted at the hotel like long lost cousins. The name of the hotel, I am sorry to say, along with other names of places irrelevant to the telling of my story, is just a jot in my mind.

I remember it being in the Theatre District close enough for Eve and I to wander over to Drury Lane where the costermongers were dragging a flower cart alongside the fishmongers and other cart pushers, all begging you to buy something in a sing-song chorus as you walked across the court. A little old lady, shawls tied under her chin to ward off the cold wind, left her stationary spot and came close up to us, wafting a bunch of violets temptingly under our noses, singing "Who'll buy my violets? Just smell my pretty violets. Only tu'pence a bunch, luv. You buy my violets?" She wore clogs and a long, dark skirt covered with a white apron and what looked to be a man's jacket, all tattered and torn. Her smile, I'm sure, was a practiced art as she pinned the bunch of tiny, purple flowers onto my coat lapel and whispered, "They'ull bring ye luck tha knows, luv!" The smile stayed with me among the violets until they all wilted, and I had to let them go.

The Last War, a one-act play written by Norman Holland, an executive director of the Crosfield soap factory, dwelt on the assumption there could be a last war, and in that season of 1936 with German's Hitler and his plans for power stretching diplomatic relations to the edge of yet another war could unfortunately steam into a universal holocaust in spite of Mr. Chamberlain's well intended and dignified approach as he duly attempted, umbrella in hand, to persuade a maniac like Hitler to behave like a gentleman. Holland's imagination has the human race eradicated from the universe in the throes of war, leaving only animals fending for themselves and portrayed on stage by the Crosfield drama team. We played the monkey, the leopard, and a couple more species. I was the lion, and our Eve was a snake in the Garden of Eden wound around the apple tree.

Eventually we, too, all vanished from the earth, leaving only the microbe and the angel who read from his holy book. And I can't remember a word that he said.

The coveted cup we had won that night was presented at a prestigious banquet in a posh hotel. Was it the Ritz? Or the Waldorf Astoria? As one grows older, one can't be bothered with trivialities and names of places, even famous and important places have become unimportant in my life.

Anyway, in the seventy odd years that have gone by, Mother, here I am still standing, whereas both those grand hotels may have since gone the way of all old buildings, down in the dust.

What I do remember, vividly, is that our happy gang of prizewinners, along with the losing companies' competitors, had received an invitation to dine with the founding father of Unilever Limited, Lord Leverhulme himself, and that the elegance of the occasion was fit for a king, though his majesty wasn't there. Still, I didn't miss a beat of that wonderful evening, even though at that time in my life, I didn't know the difference between damask and a demitasse!

Just in case I should make a wrong move, I buried my face behind the menu, which I found to my dismay was written in French. Eve saved the day for me, and with a rather superior air to show off her knowledge of the language, she picked up her menu and rattled off a few words, translating them to mean table d'hôte, the chef's choice, which meant I would be eating de boeuf, and there was no need to request the waiter for beef, please. "Guess what's for dessert?" Eve asked, looking up with a smile. I had already spotted that one on the list, and it was my turn to smile. Didn't everybody know that cherries jubilee was a flamboyant presentation, something topped with cherries that had soaked in brandy, aux-de-vie, if you please, which the waiters would set alight on their trays before parading them high above their heads as they moved from table to table around the room. I must have read that somewhere. I had certainly never tasted cherries jubilee.

The soup had not yet been served when one of the dozen or so waiters who lined the mirrored walls waltzed out of line, dodging chair legs and their human counterparts. He minced his way through the maze of tables, a look of haughty servitude painted on his face and a spotless white serviette, lovingly draped over the sleeve of his black dinner jacket, waiting to be flipped out to serve the slightest request from his lordship. His image reflected from those four mirrored walls looked like a plethora of penguins with sore feet.

My sister broke my thoughts into shivers of apprehension as she nudged me and said, "He's coming to our table." And he most certainly was. He handed me a note, and I nervously wondered if I had made a faux pas somewhere along the line of introductions to his lordship or if his honor had noticed a petticoat showing or a ladder running up my tights. It was not often that a commoner dined and supped with the aristocracy. In those days formality overshadowed any hint of familiarity, and I felt somewhat uncomfortable in my little black dress, with not a glimmer of glitter about it to show I had any right to be there.

And there the waiter stood, hand outstretched, and I almost swooned as he took a slip of paper from the silver tray and offering it, bent down and whispered in my ear, "You are Miss Eva Hope, aren't you?" My sigh of relief let out wind enough to blow out the candle in the centerpiece, and words failed me as I shook my head and pointed to my sister. She grabbed the note, staring in disbelief, and said, "Wow, I've been invited to sit with his lordship!"

Waving the waiter aside, she pushed back her own chair and sailed majestically over to the head table to take her place of honor behind the potted palms. I was left high and dry to contemplate the dozen pieces of cutlery and a like amount of various shaped and sized pieces of crystal from which to sip the drinks that were right for each and every course on the menu. I felt a strong desire to dive under the table before I fell under it after raising them in toasts to the king, even though he wasn't there. I suppose our founding father, the most eminent lord, had taken a fancy to our Eve for her portrayal of the snake slithering around the tree in the Garden of Eden as the archangel proclaimed the doom of man at the last trump of "The Last War" with the microbe character standing at his side.

The applause was enough to bring the house down, and our Eve was loving it. Or more probably, he had fallen madly in love with her since she was the image of Deanna Durbin, one of the most beautiful movie stars of the era.

The plant pots had been cleared away in case his worship wanted to rest his elbows on the table, and I could see Eve, fork in left hand hovering midway to mouth, right hand grasping something like a megaphone, which I guessed was an ear trumpet through which my sister would speak to her companion.

She looked like a contortionist trying to act as a lady accustomed to conversing with the crème de la crème of society, and at the same time maintaining equilibrium and dignity. Our Eve rose to the occasion, as always, managing a difficult situation in a manner befitting her dramatic accomplishments. And so did his lordship as he stood and praised her performance, his beard scratching a gusty kiss on her cheek while handing her the winners' trophy in our behalf. Of course she took the kind of bows befitting Lady Peel (Beatrice Lillie), queen of comediennes, and daring to blow me a kiss in recognition of my presence. And all I had to do was sit back, tuck in, and say nothing more than, "Pass the salt, please."

All in all it was a grand celebration and a fabulous meal, one far from the fish and chips to which we were accustomed. When the dinner was all but done, that same smiling waiter who'd brought Eve the note wobbled over to my table, silver tray held high, ready to serve the flaming dessert. And he had the audacity to wink at me.

The next time he made the rounds, a new serviette folded over his wrist, he asked, "Black or white, madam?" I had no idea what he meant by black or white, but thought I had better choose one of the two since the wine was making me sleepy, so I said, "White, please," glad that I made that choice when he picked up a pitcher filled with hot milk and poured in half a cup of that before filling the rest of the cup with the black coffee. I passed him my best smile with another sigh as he went on with his silver pots to the diner next to me. "Black or white, ma'am?"

I took another sip from my cup of white coffee, but all I wanted at that moment was our little cottage on Gatewarth Street and a nice hot cup of mother's Mazawattee tea. Our Eve was a star that summer night of 1936. A new century has already begun, and I am still waiting to be discovered. And, no, I have still not stopped dreaming.

CHAPTER IV

WAITING AND WONDERING

The Yanks are coming. The Yanks are coming!

Was that a thunderbolt dropped from clouds overhead? No just Neville Chamberlain folding up his umbrella with a decisive snap, announcing there was no hope of future peace talks with a madman such as Hitler and that Britain was destined to be at war. This story might bring tears to your eyes, Mother, because when you have lived through a war knocking at your door, be it a skirmish quickly ended or the hundred-year battle with France or the War of the Roses pitting Lancaster against York in England, fighting for sovereign representation between those two shires Lancashire and Yorkshire, whether the ruling of jolly old England should be in the name of the Catholic or Episcopalian religion, you wonder why, with all past history before us, why on earth have we not learned to keep peace in our time.

I was nineteen and my older sister twenty-one. Two preteen sisters, Mother, and Father, made up our happy family. We had no brothers, and that was the first thing Mother said when she heard the frightening word "war" from a man whose purpose in leading a country was devoted to keeping peace in our time.

The year was 1941. More thought went into the decision to date an American serviceman than was necessary, since we loved them all for the sacrifice of leaving home and families to come to the aid of the Brits. Mother would say over and over, "Now don't you get ideas in your head, young lady, of going out with those Yankees. In no time at all, they will have won this war for us, and then what? Of course, they will be shipped back home! And then what? You'll be shipping out there, too, will you?"

I daren't look her in the eye, because I had heard old wives' tales about streets of gold, a chicken in every pot, plus a car and a boat in every garage over there.

"But Heaven be praised that you are not boys, and you should be thankful for that," she added.

Mother would take in a sharp breath, looking up at a picture on the kitchen wall of a young soldier dressed to kill in the First World War, rifle in hand and a packsack on his back.

When Armistice Day rolled around each year to commemorate that heart-wrenching World War I in her younger days, I always wondered why Mother would ask me to kneel before that picture with her to observe the two-minute silence ceremony. In those days we wondered about a lot of things, even family affairs, because the answer to our questions always would be: "Children should be seen and not heard." Another caution would be: "It is none of your business now, is it, luv?"

But war is our business. It affects us no matter how young or how old we are or how personally it has touched our lives. I hope that our knowledgeable young people today are questioning the history of war, as they become leaders of a new generation beyond my time. I hope leaders have more sense and responsibility than to engage our country uninvited into combat that has been never-ending in the sands of time.

More than ever today, the threat of mass destruction hanging over the world should shake us out of complacency, not ready to win or lose in the battle, but to look back in history and more conscientiously study necessity versus consequence in presidential decisions to rush senselessly into warfare that has little prospect of achieving peace.

Looking back on those troubled times in our war-torn England, ration coupons were more valuable than all the gold Hitler was confiscating and secretly shoveling underground for posterity.

Life does go on, however, and we take what comes, trying to bear up under the pressure of depression. It was really no sacrifice to eat sparingly and to wear our clothes until they wore out, because coupons didn't quite cover everything we needed, but there was nothing worth cooking anyhow because of the meager rations allowed per person.

Actually all I knew about cookery in my childhood was that potatoes were made into chips and bread into *pobs*. Mother's home cooking had neither rhyme nor reason, especially during the depressing strike and strife years of the '20s and '30s when Father and millions of other men were unemployed throughout the depression. We had to be satisfied with yucky brown bread for breakfast, chips for dinner, and chips for tea.

I would hear you say, Mother, "Well, if we can't do, we'll just have to do without now, won't we?" And so the feeling of poverty during the holocaust was just like the good old days of the '20s and '30s, the depression years, to the Hope family.

The oceans were still swimming over with fish in 1939, and that tasty dish, mercifully, was not rationed, but if Mother fancied a little salmon or perch for Father's tea, she had to queue up for two or more hours early mornings at the market. Whereupon, finally reaching the butcher's block, she would hear the fishmonger wife's singsong voice rising in question.

"Well, what'll it be today, luv?" as she cut off a hunk from a fast dwindling heap of Atlantic's bountiful codfish. Mother would dare to say, "I'd like a nice piece of Dover sole, please."

"This all the catch we got!" The woman sneered, slapping the smelly cod on to a page of the *Manchester Guardian* and into mother's shopping basket with a sniff, a sigh, and a "'ere y'ar then, luv. There's plenty more where that come from, and i'nt it nice, luv, all without coupons."

My friends and I used make-up cream to cover our legs, a stand-in for stockings, when coupons didn't stretch far enough to cover their purchase.

Mother had suffered in World War I, and long ago she had learned to "make do," and often when things were at their lowest ebb, we would hear her singing a marching song from memories of her loved ones who had never come home from that First World War. We would kick up our heels in a march around the kitchen table, stamping our feet to emphasize the beat of the words as she sang.

Pack up your troubles in your old kit bag
And smile, smile, smile.
While there's a Lucifer to light your fag,
Smile boys that's the style.
What's the use of worrying
It never was worthwhile
So ...
Pack all your troubles in your old kit bag
And smile, smile, smile.

American troops landed on our shores soon after Churchill and Roosevelt agreed that a madman such as Hitler would stop at nothing to overcome Britain, and the USA would be his next stop, unless his super-star dreams turned into nightmares and he woke up in a pile of gold dust.

A sigh of relief went around our land for those brave men and women who had come to our rescue from a country so far away as America, many to lose their lives for the sake of such as I. There aren't too many Brits still living from that horrendous era. I am one of the fortunate, surviving the rations, the raids, and the rubble while dreaming of a country over there with its so-called freedoms of which I had no inkling.

Whenever I think of you, Mother, getting up early to stand in line at the fish market early mornings, it brings back the night that Grandmother Hope came to visit us along with a group of American airmen she had never met before that fateful evening.

The boys had been driving lorries in a convoy down the highway, scarcely able to see a hand before their eyes in a blackout along with fog and not even a moon to guide them. Every window in Britain was, by law, wearing black covers to shut out the light from our homes so that the next bombarding would go whistling in the wind, and we could go back to bed.

The drivers were about to pull off the road when the hazy bit of light flickering ahead, which they presumed was another brave soul driving the highway, was the only thing that kept them moving on, hopefully, to their destination.

Without warning, the light wavered a little and then seemed to be flashing signals at short intervals, so the airmen carefully guided their vehicles to the curb and made their way on foot to investigate the cause of the flashing SOS.

They couldn't believe their eyes, but a skinny old lady had been guiding them with her blackout flashlight! It was Grandmother Mary Elizabeth Hope, trying to find her way home and thinking she was on the sidewalk.

And here she was, a heroine guiding army vehicles carrying ammunition and supplies on a dark, foggy night when a woman her age should be home in bed. How they found our house is still a mystery. We were too shocked to think of asking.

We made the boys welcome and thanked them for rescuing Grandmother, then, as Mother finished serving them a cup of tea with chips, she turned to Father and said,

"'Arold, will you knock me up early in the morning, luv. I have to go queue up at the fish market if you want fish for your tea."

Those American boys couldn't contain themselves on hearing such a question spoken so seriously from a sedately proper English lady, and their laughter was loud enough to bring down the Nazis from their mission overhead to join in the fun. But Mother turned beet red, gave them a puzzled stare, and turned on her heel heading for the stairs.

I felt embarrassed along with you, Mother, because I didn't understand their laughter either. It was a good thing our Ike had been working with the American Forces at Burtonwood and understood there was a sexual meaning to those words, so she called after Mother, "It's all right, luv; they weren't laughing at you. That was an old American saying that everyone understands over there."

This same phrase—knocked up—has an entirely different connotation in proper English. It was used over there long before Edison's 1878 discovery of the phonograph and hence the telephone. With no other means of communication between railroad supervisors and their workers, young boys with bicycles were hired to ride to the homes of train engineers where they would loudly bang the door knockers to make sure the crews were up and about in time to meet their obligation to run on schedule—knocking them up, if you please!

I met my husband at the YMCA while serving him a cup of coffee on my weekly stint of wartime home duty. He was the most insistent man I had ever met. Week after week, cup after cup, he would almost beg to take me to a movie. There was a sadness in his eyes, which finally persuaded me to go, in spite of Mother's warning.

The movie was about the cowboys and Indians, and the movie house was nicknamed the Blood Tub because the movies were violent, and it only cost two pennies per ticket admission.

Our wedding took place in Warrington, Lancashire, in September 1943. Deeply indebted to generous relatives and friends, I offered up thankful prayers as they showered me with their own precious coupons to purchase a wedding trousseau. Mrs. Delaney used her own food stamps and graciously offered food rations from her family to make a beautifully decorated cake.

You reminded me, Mother, about the tiny white decorative boxes I would need to hold a bite or two of the cake intended for my girl friends to take home with them. She had insisted it was tradition and that each of those spinsters should put their boxes of wedding cake under their pillows that night and make a wish for a husband as handsome as mine. You took care of every small detail at my wedding, Mother, even though I would be going out of your life, perhaps forever.

But many of those young ladies realized the futility of them catching a bride's bouquet to ensure they would become the next spinster to be married. How could they dream of parading down the aisle while their sweethearts were marching, guns at the ready to kill?

In my younger days, a wedding was a wedding, and almost sanctified as such, but living together or common law marriage were definitely a sacrifice of good reputation as an upstanding or outstanding citizen. So naturally most young women claimed the right to a real wedding, with parental permission of course, to be married in full glory before God's anointed clergy in long-ago established church rites before the Benedictine Monks became leaders of the English Protestant movement, gaining importance in Chester Cathedral near my home town of Warrington.

Such established wedding vows during wartime, however, were almost a flight of fancy. Beautiful white dresses gathered dust in store windows while promises of bliss were postponed until peace came down to earth once more and rations coupons went out of control, a relief for everyone whose hopes of buying anything new were just about burned out, because a new coat alone would cost almost the whole book of twenty-four clothes rations coupons.

Amazingly my wedding turned out to be a posh affair. Stemming from their love, friendship, indebtedness, or the stuff that brings people together during hard times, my family and friends gave up their precious clothes ration coupons so that I might be outfitted for a church wedding.

Those loving people who had sacrificed their coupons assured me I should use any leftovers for my honeymoon, and I already knew what they would purchase.

Saddened by the thought of losing lifelong acquaintances, I realized the impossibility of any one of my family or friends making that hazardous trip to the United States with me during wartime, or being able to afford it if and whenever the war ended, so I devised a scheme to imprint their names into my heart for all time.

With thoughts racing ahead of me, I bought four three-square yards of Irish linen and feather and stitched them together so as to form a six-foot square dining tablecloth. I took great care, pulling out six horizontal strands of thread from two inches inside the linen's perimeter and hem-stitching the remaining vertical threads into a fancy border to complete the cloth, now ready for family and friends to sign over their lives to me so they could be embroidered in colored thread and live on forever.

So you see, I never really left all of those people shedding tears back there in England when I sailed to America on a cold January day in 1945.

You told me it was a lovely idea and reminded me to add new friends to it.

I listened to you, Mother, and today, in 2012, almost fifty years later, there are more than five hundred names surrounding our family's names in the center.

My daughter Hope will be embroidering future signatures, since my sight no longer accommodates threading a needle. I can barely see the needle, let alone thread anything through its eye.

CHAPTER V

A CALL TO ALMS

To call war the soil of courage and virtue
Is like calling debauchery the soil of love.
—George Santayana
In peace, sons bury their fathers. In war, fathers bury their sons.
—Herodotus

"Bring him home ... Bring him home ..."

I still listen to that particular recording of *Les Miserable* when I feel sad, and the haunting notes—bring him home, bring him home—go out into space as I sing along with the music and a man's glorious voice to speak my own deep-down feelings on the heartbreaking crunch of warmongering.

Soon after the wedding, my husband announced the startling news that he had requested of his squadron commander that I be one of the first wives to be sent overseas to his home in Polson, Montana, until he could join me there. I was somewhat shaken up by the news that I might be traveling alone, so I didn't dwell on the possibility that it might happen before the war ended.

But life does go on no matter what we cook up or what we write down so long as we keep on writing and never have to eat our words.

Life can also go at a snail's pace, especially during a war while awaiting emigration to the United States as a British war bride, with nothing worth cooking anyway to offset meager rations.

A glimpse into a future where I may never again see people I loved and respected led me to shove my cookbooks into a bottom drawer until cooking ingredients were more plentiful.

I then spent more time fire watching for incendiary bombs dropped by enemy planes during the night to light up the intended area pinpointed for their big bombs. That procedure took two people working together: one operating the extinguisher and the other partner running forward to lie on the road holding the hose nozzle pointed at the sizzling incendiary bomb about to burst into flames if my partner and I didn't get there first.

I might also do extra duty cooking at the YMCA at teatime. The evening hours I could take advantage of Red Cross classes to gain more knowledge of poisonous gases and emergency care for casualties on the home front. As the rage of war blazed across the English Channel, blitzing whatever took its fancy, our guns were no match for the enemy. But there I was, planning to run away from it all and maybe into a never-never land. I never imagined you cared that I was leaving behind everything and everybody that I loved, but I saw the anguish in your face as you were waving good-bye from the quayside, and I was trembling with uncertainty when you turned and walked slowly away.

I could never know until now, a widow at ninety-one, and you, Mother, a treasured name on my linen tablecloth, how you really suffered in your stoic hold on life, especially when our Eve came over here with her American airman. All the solace I can offer now, Mother, is the wisdom of philosopher Horace who wrote: "They change their climate, not their souls who rush across the seas."

Chapter VI

CROSSING THE ATLANTIC

In January of 1945 I was among some of those gallant Americans who were actually going home to their families as casualties from the inhumanity of war. As a British war bride, my husband wanted to be sure I sailed to America and had submitted my name to be one of the first to be emigrated, believing he was due to a furlough and could come with me.

I passed the emigration steps with flying colors, but his leave became tangled up in red tape, and he had to wait in England for the remainder of the war while I traveled across America to Polson, Montana, alone. A challenge for anyone in World War II when men in uniform were anxious to be on leave as they hurried home to their families.

The first indication I was chosen to come to this country came in the form of a telephone call from the American Embassy in Liverpool. "Are you Miss Irene Hope, now married to an American citizen?" And when I confirmed that I was, she asked me if I could recite his serial number for her. I never thought I would need to remember that number so many years to this day, but #19070704 has been a sort of hesitating, repetitious marching rhythm commanding me to watch my step to the tune of my sergeant husband's chant as I traveled without him across the sea.

"Listen carefully now," the voice continued. "I can not give you any official information because of wartime protocol, but you are expected at the American Embassy in Liverpool promptly at 10:00 a.m. tomorrow. You are to tell no one you will be leaving Warrington or what this message conveys to you. You will be allowed to bring two suitcases, and be sure to mark them V-2. There will be a vehicle waiting there for you. You will be allowed to carry one hundred pounds in travelers' checks for your journey."

Could I leave my family without a word or quit my job without notification of doing so. So I confided in my mother and three sisters, who promised secrecy and assured me they would come up with something, but they were not looking forward to seeing me go away.

The *Mauritania* was a luxury liner belonging to the British company Canard Lines, on loan to the USA for the use of transporting troops and supplies during those war years.

I was one of the first few war brides who were also westward bound with the war still blasting away. Fear was everywhere. You couldn't see it or hear it, but you could feel it running up and down the spine as you navigated that once luxurious vessel now void of all its trimmings and serving as a hospital ship for wounded casualties.

Before our ship set out to sea, the brides who were ocean bound were anxiously waiting on board at Liverpool Harbor, locked out from sea and shore by fog that was a real blindfold swirling its way in and around the ship before sneaking out and spreading over the harbor to the sea.

During those fear-filled days, we fretted that none of our relatives knew where we were or if our vessel had been torpedoed leaving home. We could not communicate with the British until we had reached the shores of America. And if you had the habit of smoking cigarettes, you weren't allowed to light up on top deck throughout the long, silent blacked-out nights.

The tugboats' crews had given up any hope of piloting the largest vessel allowed to leave the Liverpool docks, and the fog hung around until it wore itself out, giving those tugboats the awesome task of guiding that queenly cruise ship into an ocean where Hitler's submarines were prowling below, ready and eager to deliver their torpedoes. That doesn't calm the nerves one bit, and I was wishing you were there, Mother, to bear the burden with me.

No matter how I tried to look ahead with promises of a rose garden and a happy family while tossing and turning on an upper bunk aboard the *Mauritania*, my mind was dragged back again and again to what I had left in limbo. One thing only brought compensation. I wouldn't need coupon books from that day forward.

I slid down from a top bunk in a refitted luxury stateroom on the *Mauretania* and into the worn-out, leather brogues with the cute leather acorn tags dangling from the laces. Mother had insisted I buy the shoes because they were serviceable, which they had been in spite of cold feet sans stockings, because coupons never stretched far enough to purchase stockings.

I survived that trip to America, determined to hang on to my faith, so I visited the American casualties who shared their own hopes for the future with stories from beds in cabins stripped of luxury to facilitate their continuing medial care.

They held back tears, telling their longing to be back in their big cities and small towns in America the beautiful, home of the free. I felt their longing to be home again in a country they loved. One or two young men shared the news that they were going home to hug babies who were not yet born when they were called into service. Most of them produced pictures of loved ones eagerly awaiting their homecoming.

And they teased me about the way I pronounced Montaaaana and said all they raised out there were sheep and shepherds. They also taught me how to play cribbage and pinochle.

Wandering around the rails of the upper deck, submarines submerging in my mind, I felt more reassured when a crew member notified me to listen for the boat muster drill signal, where it was mandatory to wear my lifebelt and head for my particular lifeboat during the exercise. He also warned me that a sub had been spotted on our path during the night.

In the middle of the Atlantic Ocean, I desperately wanted to swim back to what was old and familiar, but compelled to steam ahead to what was new and strange.

What I needed most, dear Mother, was you.

All I really wanted was a nice, hot cup of your home-brewed tea and a train ticket to Montana, or, even more so, a way back home. But as the *Mauritania* sailed ever closer to her destination, I thought I was about to see a riot aboard. People were rushing to the ship's rail, pushing and shoving, and I felt myself carried along with the crowd, some of them hobbling along on crutches, some in wheelchairs spinning around crazily.

"There she is! See, over this way! No, over here …" Someone had spotted the lady with the lamp.

Their Statue of Liberty was welcoming them home, and I became one of them. What a homecoming, even though I was leaving my home behind. What a welcome for a stranger to witness. They were home, and I felt as though I was being pushed through an open door, at one with them. They gave me faith in their motherland, which I hoped to call mine.

Chapter VII

THE BIG APPLE

Not that I was ever considered cowardly, but I had heard so many thumbs-up stories about Uncle Sam and his zealous citizens and the good old American way that I feel somewhat unqualified to take on America as I stepped gingerly down the gangplank to mark my first footsteps on the shores of my promised land.

Feeling a trifle sickly, as though waking up from an everlasting moment of fear, I sat paralyzed in time and space on a suitcase marked V-2, three thousand miles away from home, not yet realizing there were many mores to go, alone into the vast unknown, with a tired, foggy mind, and muttering to myself, "Now, what do I do?"

I glanced over at the other gangway, where men in uniform were jostling one another for room to run, or hobble on their crutches, into the waving, outstretched arms of their loved ones. Cheering, laughing couples kissed and kissed again; elderly men and women reached for their returning sons and daughters; large families bunched around one of their own; and I wondered about a long and lanky young man, the one with his face buried inside the blanket, obviously protecting a newborn child from the blustery winter winds. So tightly in his arms, it seemed as if he would never let go. I wondered which he might be of the many returning heroes who were swept up in the joy of holding a son or daughter for the very first time.

I was tempted to approach one of those many rejoicing people to ask, "Where should I go? Tell me. Point out my way. Anywhere!"

I fought back the urge to intrude, reluctant to interrupt their joy with such a down-to-earth question, and instead followed the last one of the English girls who looked as though she knew where she was going.

It was to Customs, where loads of luggage had been tossed onto the ground, and suitcases were lying open as uniformed officials checked their contents for contraband. The English woman headed for the end of the long row of frustrated travelers, and I was fortunate to find an empty space right away as a Customs officer impatiently grabbed my bags and waited for my turn to declare whether or not I had brought a bit of jolly old England along with me.

Finally my own V-2s were thrown open and carelessly ransacked while I stood there, still in a stupor, a wad of travelers' checks for a train ticket clutched in my hand, knowing only that I was maybe standing on streets of faux gold, wishing I had some of the real coin in my pocket and wondering what on earth I would do next. At the same time, praying the gentleman would not consider Granny Hope's cup and saucer present—Royal Doulton, Glamis Thistle pattern.

And then I saw one smiling face I shall remember forever, Mother. The man came over to the baggage area and pointed to my luggage. "Could you use a little help here?" he asked. With a deep sigh of relief, the words came out, "Oh, thank you! YES!" and must have seemed out of all proportion to that simple question. As I accepted the card he held out, I breathed a sigh of relief the Lady with the Lamp must have heard. The kind gentleman was a Red Cross representative who took me under his wing and escorted me back to his headquarters, where I sat for several hours while he tried to book a train reservation to Montana. I soon discovered there were no reservations readily available since members of the US Forces had right of way to travel during the war. But thankfully the Red Cross had been promised a berth for me the following day.

Quickly assessing my look of dismay, he asked whether I had money enough to stay overnight, and when I shook my head, saying I was only allowed to take one hundred dollars out of my country and did not know how much the cost of the westbound trip would be, he phoned in a reservation anyway, at some hotel, the name long since forgotten, the cost to be taken care of by the Red Cross.

Until then I was free to roam the streets and get a taste of the Big Apple. But first I had to find my way to the lift. I had walked down several staircases before the word elevator sunk in as going up; therefore, it must also come down.

Today I would be delighted by the chance for a one-day visit to the Big Apple, seeing the sights, the shops, the shows. But there, on the sidewalks of New York almost sixty years ago, home was still the England I had forsaken, and my dreams of a home in faraway Montana, the Land of Shining Mountains dreamed of by my father, were still a long way from being realized.

New York City was a strange and somewhat terrifying ordeal. Hailing a taxi with the grace and aplomb of film star Paulette Goddard would have been difficult enough, even in the best of times and in a familiar city. Only a fool or a foreigner would try to hail a cab on the wrong side of Madison Avenue! I wasn't born a fool, neither was I born and raised in America, but I certainly felt like a fool when I realized the right side of the road to travel in America *is* the right side of the road and not the left, as it was in England.

Wondering why the citizens of that huge metropolis seemed in such a big hurry along its sidewalks, I quickly found out. There was just too much of it to swallow in one gulp.

In the city, time becomes visible.
—Mumford

I cashed in my travelers' checks, and with a little money in my pocket for accidental or incidental surprises and much trepidation, I found myself westward ho to the land of sheep and shepherds. But that's another story, and I'll let you think on the past, Mother, while I write to you about the ups and downs of my years as an American citizen to the age of ninety-one.

Ray died ten years ago, after a long siege of Alzheimer's disease, Mother, but I remembered your stiff upper lip when Father died and took a lesson from that.

CHAPTER VIII

JOY AND SORROW

When you have a granddaughter excitedly planning for her wedding, you can't possibly stand by without saying, "Is there something I can do?" even if she lives on the East Coast in Rhode Island, and you live in the west by the Pacific Ocean in Oregon.

There was a hint of joy in her voice, and I wondered if I had said too much when she exclaimed, "Yes! We would love you to perform the ceremony!"

Well, for one thing, I was not an ordained minister of the church but merely a lay speaker. Even so, living in an era today where anything goes, the pristine rites of the Church of England still tug at my conscience defiantly keeping a hold on the past, so I declined her request. However, I did offer to say a few words after the knot was tied and the bride-to-be and her intended were pacified.

The wedding was planned to be in Montana, where Molly was born and had lived close to Glacier National Park most of her life. The auditorium was situated outdoors on the shores of McDonald Lake, amid Montana's glaciers.

As she spoke that day on the telephone, I was remembering the Mission Range in Flathead Count, Montana, in 1945, their grandeur taking my breath away as the rickety old mountain bus skidded along the icy road at a caterpillar crawl. The weather was twenty degrees below zero, and I was a strange in a new world of uncertainty, hoping for a warm breath of welcome along the shores of Flathead Lake.

The person sitting next to me was a quiet Indian lady. She spoke just once or twice, asking me where I had found the pheasant feather in my hat and a remark about my bare legs. I think we could have sat there in silent communion forever. I was sorry to see her get off the bus a few miles before I did, at St. Ignatius, another tiny town snuggled up to those silent mountains. The uncle met me at the drug store in Polson then drove slowly in the old Ford until we reached a steep hill at the bend in the highway as it turned north following the lake along its eastern shore.

In those days, safe driving depended on circumstance, especially when you hear the words "hang on, she's sliding back down again." Safety belts and air bags were not in vogue, and if I had my way, we might as well have slid back all the way to New York City.

The log cabin atop that slippery slope looked foreboding beneath the darkening sky, and my hopes for a warm welcome were shattered as I walked into the kitchen where a pot-bellied woodstove was belting out its heat in a warm welcome.

"Oh, you finally got here, huh? Here's a chair. Sit yourself down, and we'll teach you to play pinochle." I didn't feel it was my duty to tell them some lonely souls aboard ship had already taught me the game of pinochle, but when I shared the realization that I may be expecting our first child, the aunt threw up her hands in disgust and a big sneer was taking over her unctuous smile.

"Does my nephew know about this?" When I reasoned there was no phone in her home, I could see her anger mounting in the narrowing of her eyes as she muttered between her teeth, "Who knows—the kid might not be his! Why couldn't Ramie have married a nice young girl from around here and not a foreigner from some other country?"

I was hurt enough to shoot back at her, "If you think I was jollying around on any weary trip across an ocean or sneaking off the train at some lonely spot overland, you've got another think coming, and if those thoughts concern my character, you'll be eating them before you can spit them out!"

I didn't believe in cursing and had never used the word damn before, so I muttered it under my breath to myself, "Damn her." It felt good.

I stayed simply because there was nowhere else to go at that point, but the outburst revived the old British spirit, nagging me to find a job and at least get away from the relatives for a while.

It didn't seem to be happening to me, but the next morning found me sliding down the steep icy hill on my bum and waiting for the school bus to come chugging along, hoping the driver would give me a lift into town to find a job.

I stood, looking up at the snow-covered Mission Mountains taking in their mighty presence, rising up from the foothills behind the barn at the top of the hill where

I now lived.

They were so close at that moment that I imagined if I reached out my hand I could touch them and know them as a fortress guarding me from harm. And if I dared, I would steal from them a bit of their strength to see me through another day, a bit of their endurance to help me bear the pain of loneliness, and from their lofty peaks a bit of their virgin snows, untouched by the world below, to urge me on to heights I one day might possibly go.

A whiff of foul-smelling skunk cabbage pushing its way up through the snow floated by, and I come down to earth again, glad to be gone for most of the day from the place up the hill I could never call home.

The bus honked its arrival, and the driver giving me a skeptical look said, "Hop in!"

I hopped off at the drug store, where I bought a newspaper, circled an ad, and made my way on foot to find the law office of Lloyd Wallace who was also a senator for Lake County. I worked for him until the day my son was born.

It was impossible to dream then that the child I expected would one day have a daughter, Molly, who was now asking me on the telephone to conduct her wedding vows.

Standing between the bride and groom, Molly and Jaime on stage at their wedding day in 2007, Lake McDonald and the glorious glacier country beyond, I shared with them my thoughts and feelings on that soul-filling emotion I found very early in my life while racing across a field to pick a posy. I could feel the emotion of it then and knew that it was joy.

"A kindred soul of mine ends all her e-mail with the message: "Don't Postpone Joy." It sounds very fitting when you first think on it, until you analyze the *possibility* of how this thought-provoking *probability* could ever be accomplished by anyone, especially an octogenarian going on ninety, with the lust turning to dust and a racing heartbeat settling down into a pony trot. Who can define what really is a *joy*, ready and eager to say to the moment? Who could even think of postponing such emotion if it were ever possible to do so? It is not some electrically charged gadget you can put by with your umbrella for a rainy day.

My joy has always followed its own bliss and appears instantaneously on serendipitous occasions.

For instance, the other day that emotion popped up on the Scrabble board, J-O-Y, and lo and behold, when I placed my last four tiles, A-N-C-E, there was the seldom-used word, J-O-Y-A-N-C-E— all I needed to win the game.

Oh, what a wonderful feeling the love of language imparts to such moments. A tiny taste of pure and simple JOY!

Postpone it? Not on you life. A little of that fulfilling feeling comes flying by and I swallow it whole. I admit my exuberance over that small challenge is somewhat unfounded, but you will understand when you are pushing ninety, you don't go chasing rainbows every day.

Challenges, big and small, bring the excitement of joyance into my life, and if I were home, I'd be tempted to try another slam or two at bridge before calling today a night.

But it *is* still the little bits of joy in life that might sneak up and take your breath away.

I shall always remember a young boy with the signs of Down's syndrome sitting next to me while waiting for the city bus one day, and I offered him a piece of the candy bar I was unwrapping. His apparent love for chocolate led me to ask if he would like a bar all to himself to take home, and with a nod of the head and a whoop of appreciation, up from his seat he wrapped his arms around my neck, planting a big, sloppy kiss on my cheek. He awkwardly stuffed the bar into his jacket pocket and shouted, "I'm going to show this to EVERYBODY WHEN I GET HOME!"

It's those little, unexpected things that make you cry for joy. It has also sought me out in the solitude of living alone, reverberating from the haunting notes of Rachmaninoff's *Theme of Paganini*, played as only Ashkenazy's talents prove, in time and melody as the composer intended. I listen and wait in vain for my husband's rocking chair nearby to make an empty move and keep in time with his death and the reality of it all. I am overcome by the emotions of longing the music conveys, soothing loneliness and bringing peaceful solitude where joy may become more than a three-letter word in my life.

I can never purposely predict it, nor deliberately postpone those precious moments to just another day, but the door will always be open to that sweet mystery of life called joy. I christen your new life together with words of wisdom from a prophet more poetic than I shall ever be, coming straight from the heart of Khalil Gibran.

In his book *The Prophet*, the seeress Almitra is questioning Almustafa, the chosen one, to share his wisdom before leaving The City of Orphalese.

And I pray that your married lives be *forever* guided by these words:

Almitra spoke again and said, And what of Marriage, master?
And he answered saying:
You were born together, and together you shall be forevermore.
You shall be together when the white wings of death scatter your days.
Ay, you shall be together
even in the silent memory of God.
But let there be spaces in your togetherness,
And let the winds of the Heavens dance between you.
Love one another, but make not a bond of love:
Let it rather be a moving sea between the shores of your souls.
Fill each other's cup but drink not from one cup.
Give one another of your bread but eat not from the same loaf.
Sing and dance together and be joyous, but let each one of you be alone,
Even as the strings of a lute are alone though they quiver with the same music.
Give your hearts, but not into each other's keeping.
For only the hand of Life can contain your hearts.
And stand together yet not too near together:
For the pillars of the temple stand apart,
And the oak and the cyprus
grow not in each other's shadow.

May you both live a long and happy life together and may each of your two cups bubble over with joy.

If the sun and moon should ever doubt, they would go out.
—William Blake

You and I may be too old to dig for gold, but there are more valuable treasures than gold within our reach.

We can dig down deep within our hearts for one thing and find that forgiving was the precursor to forgetting the cuts and bruises it may have suffered along the way.

We remember that patience has been a virtue as we raised our children, the reward for that patience shining out from the happy, smiling faces of our grandchildren.

And as we have been touched by the fleeting ecstasy of joy throughout our lives, we understand that the pangs of your game rises to a whopping forty points over Maven's level. Not this dreamer! A little of that heavenly feeling comes flying by, and I swallow it whole as my score creeps higher over one thousand each blessed day. I admit my exuberance is somewhat unfounded, but you know, my computer competitor, Maven, cheats! She adds 'aitches where there aren't any and challenges my perfectly spelled words without giving me the option to question the ridiculous plural suffixes she adds on to my singular nouns and verbs, even adverbs and adjectives.

Succeeding over a computer's challenges brings the excitement of joyance into my life, and I'm tempted to try another slam or two at bridge, too, before calling the day a night.

But seriously, it really is the little things that have helped me take a grasp on joy, the surprising serendipity of it knocking at my door, helping me hang on to things. Like the tiny, white bundle of fur my son handed me on his way to university. "Here, Mom," he says, "you'll be needing something to hang on to now that we are all off to college, something to love and live for!"

"Oh no! Not a dog," I whimper to myself. But, yes, it was a dog, and by no means a cuddly lap dog like friend Dorothy's Mr. Chips. I couldn't exactly hang onto this little bundle of joy, because she grew up with leaps and bounds into a 210-pound, people-loving Saint Bernard who used to take *me* for a walk. That was exhilarating exercise, however, compared to scrubbing up daily bags full of shed hair from my hardy, knobby, old-fashioned carpet with an ancient Fuller hair brush, which activity, as you can imagine, put my knees out of joint. But then, hard work can also be an invitation to soul-filling joy, can't it? I shall always remember Krissy, bushy tail and all, knocking off a knickknack or two and greeting everyone at the door with a jump of joy and a sloppy kiss. She refused to stay outdoors after burying the bone from her daily joint of meat and finally understood she was too big to sleep with me, so she settled that issue by cuddling up on the couch to watch TV with all apparent joy.

It was twelve years later when her time came to leave us, and I swear she knew what was going to happen. She turned away from sniffing the untouched steak I had foolishly set out on the grass, trying to show her how much we adored her, and as she spotted the veterinarian walking onto the patio, she dragged her feet painfully up to my chair, resting her huge head in my lap to await her fate.

Our Krissy, our beloved Saint Bernard. We buried her that early spring day beside the patio under a bush that had never given us the pleasure of one single bloom since planting. Although a purebred, she probably was not all that saintly. She couldn't even climb the front steps, let alone the Alps on a mission of mercy with a keg around her neck. She deserved no special honor above any other dog who had died and gone to heaven. But the bush that didn't bloom, her burial spot, told me another story.

At first morning light one day, the weather warming up in the Land of Shining Mountains, I thought I spotted a red blur as I looked through the kitchen window. But a slight mist hovering above the damp patio floor to greet the sun swallowed up the bit of color I had imagined. My curiosity lingered though, and a few minutes later, I took a second glance. The mist had cleared and our Krissy tree was ablaze with deep pink blossoms, bending its boughs gracefully in recognition of my presence as I walked through the doorway to stare in wonder. And I swear I heard the breeze, as it wafted the air with its fragrance, whispering, "It's love like this that makes life eternal."

Will I, too, live to bloom on earth again, a maple tree? I take in those special moments in my life now at ninety-one as they come around the bend, the butterfly touch of a hand surprising you as it passes innocently by, conveying joyful feelings of long forgotten interludes in its wake. Perhaps a yearning too for even deeper feelings to come alive before I die.

I will always remember the outreach of a helping arm from a stranger, knowing I would never make it alone down those theatre steps, I relished over again, talking with the kind gentleman about the joy of watching *Die Fledermaus* and listening to that heart-lifting music.

Surely Father's music was a blessing to you, Mother?

I am overcome by the emotions of longing pouring through the musician's fingers, and I learn that sorrow is anam cara to joy. We have to know the depth of sorrow, whether for ourselves or others, in order to appreciate the full measure of joy for all its worth.

Joy! One of the sweetest mysteries of life
Makes me wonder about the afterlife!

WHAT PRICE LOVE

"Love, what is that," this old woman cries, glancing up at the skies. Oh, love is illusive, love is sublime, the poet quickly replies.

But can anyone really explain it to me before I die?

I met Dr. Stancliffe while working in a mental health facility. No, it wasn't for a consult! I was the intake worker; he was a visiting psychiatrist. He loved art, he loved music, and he loved the people he counseled out of their misery. He relished life and all it had to offer, and he graciously passed it along on his way.

Not like the other psychiatrist who came to visit us. After her first appointment, one of our patients said of him, "God, if I see much more of that guy, I *will* be crazy." She may have become insane.

It was the good doctor's day to come in to our facility; I was listening to the music drifting from my tape recorder. Pavarotti's voice echoed his love for music around the world.

My psychiatrist friend surprised me by saying that he knew Pavarotti very well and shared with me something I had wondered about the great tenor. When I asked about his quaint habit of holding a white handkerchief on high as if he would never let it go, he confided with a smile, "Oh, that's his little blankie." I could see how that might be. The expression of joy as he sang held the wonder and the love of a happy child.

No tears were shed on that day long ago when the famous tenor was performing live, the thunderous applause rising with his final note, with white hankie held so high above his head. It never dawned on me that man should *ever* die.

When I read that heartrending news in the morning paper, I found myself repeating over and over. Oh, no! Oh, no! Oh, nooo! His voice, reigning over the world of classic music lovers for decades, had won this heart, which now was breaking.

I cried again as I watched the adulation expressed by thousands of music lovers and lovers from his native land attending his funeral, among the celebrities and dignitaries from around the world, and showing their sadness at his passing and appreciation for what he had given. He may have left our good earth, but his voice, his dignity, and his hankie will linger long. Now, what was I saying before that? Oh, yes.

If I remember rightly, I looked at my computer five or ten minutes ago and thought I might write a story about my love life, but it never got a start. A greater love got in the way. It's always been that way. Music, dance, theatre, art, philosophy have all fit into my life as far as I have lived it to this very day. Oh, I've held a foothold on the four steps of the mystical experience of love as W. H. Auden expresses in his introduction to the *Protestant Mystics* anthology by Anne Fremantle, which Auden says are the "Vision of Dame Kind, The Vision of Eros, The Vision of Agape, and the Vision of God." Bacchus, I suppose, had an earthly right to conduct his orgiastic love rites, but sex and I had a parting of the ways long ago, while searching for truth and beauty as its disclaimer.

What wonderful things in this world today might be accomplished if the energy we expend on sex could be diverted into something more meaningful than self-gratification. And one of those supposedly impossible things could be a universal understanding of one's habits and beliefs: person-to-person, city by city, and stretching the world, country to country.

Many would declare themselves sexually handicapped when asked for that kind of sacrificial love.

What exactly, in this day and age are we to believe is true, spiritual love, when even filial or brotherly love is not forthcoming from human beings who blow themselves up with their enemy to prove themselves worthy of entry into paradise. Only a Devil God would endorse that as an afterlife worth living.

I used to go to the pictures to revel in romance when I was very young. *Rebecca*, *Love Story*, *Gone With the Wind* ...

Mother, you would never believe I recently saw a movie called *Knocked Up*. You would be flabbergasted remembering World War II, with you so innocently using those words in the English connotation of banging the knuckles on the bedroom door to waken the sleeper inside. I felt so embarrassed along with you. But that was a long time ago. This titled movie was a farce with brazen women cavorting around with a group of work shirkers, men who sit around smoking whatever they fancy when they are not paying attention to our beautiful heroine.

However one of them, the hero, visits her on full screen for the world to see what happens to make her pregnant. Mother, when the screen started to show the steps she takes to rid herself of her heavy burden, my daughter and I were brave enough to stand and leave the audience still with their eyes glued to the screen.

Producers nowadays blatantly exploit true feelings of love that count for something into easy-come, easy-go frippery relationships and supposedly real-time, knock-down movies like *Knocked Up*. Give me *Mrs. Miniver* and a beautiful garden, and I'll smell the roses.

As the sophisticated woman in the old advertisement brazenly holding a long cigarette holder would say, "We've come a long way, baby." I'm thankful for that in many respects, but it seems to me our younger generation of women sporting belly-button necklines are exploiting those hard-earned freedoms fought for by our foremothers by jumping into bed at a whim, with other intent than a good night's sleep. And I'm afraid that tomorrow's woman may even further strip the virtue of respect gained for us by those brave, outspoken women who have stuck the course for our cause in the past.

So, looking at the problem from both sides of a fig leaf, while still rooting for the weaker sex, in good humor and with a shrug of the shoulders, I repeat once more Mr. Dooley's challenge from literature, "What does a woman want iv rights whin she has priv'leges?"

CHAPTER IX

LONELINESS

Tomorrow comes so quickly now, and I tend to forget there ever was a yesterday, so I set myself up to create something beautiful tomorrow, maybe a new painting for a friend, so that I can savor those hours a little longer rather than have them slip away unnoticed, for then the mind wanders and the eyes become transfixed on the rocking chair by the fire that isn't moving now.

I chide myself and say out loud, "You are a widow. You walked away from him, and he didn't say a word. You left him lying there in a wooden box, never again to see his land of shining mountains." And the aloneness he must have suffered through those forgetting years of Alzheimer's reaches out from the empty chair and grabs me into its arms.

"He who does not enjoy solitude will not love freedom," so Schopenhauer's look at life to expresses my feelings.

You, dear Mother, never had time to admit, or willingness to share, your feelings of loneliness.

I once read a book on loneliness, and the author, Moustakas, proposes that being lonely leads to new horizons of compassion and beauty, but in those days, struggling through the middle years with children underfoot, I didn't have the time or energy apart from their needs and activities to sit and ponder over things like that.

Today I have the time, the need, and the urge to contemplate the truth in this statement by Moustakas: truth, like faith, can only be judged experientially. I pull up my mind from the chair, but the rockers keep on swaying as I turn on the stereo and set the arm for the needle to start the LP sitting on the turntable.

The pianist is Vladimir Ashkenazy in concert with André Previn and the London Symphony Orchestra, pouring out with heartrending tenderness Rachmaninoff's Rhapsody on a *Theme of Paganini*, Opus 43.

I listen, enraptured, and the loneliness becomes a shawl around my shoulders, warming up the cold within and melting into the ecstasy of solitude that can fill the soul and stir the heart to tears.

I can live and love now in solitude but will never be a stranger to loneliness.

In my long life, I have learned to listen for its voice crying in the wilderness.

I hear it whispering quietly, pleading for recognition. It echoes with a hollow groan from the trashcans of our cities, breadbox for the poverty stricken in a country of the redolent rich. It rises in a stifled scream above the merriment of teenage laughter. It falls with a muffled thud, an unanswered prayer on the cushioned pews of our churches.

I think of the abandoned youngsters throughout the world, the brave young boy expected to be a man, caring for his undisciplined brothers and baby sister who screamed when he tried to untangle the knots in her hair. There was no one else to hug her close and rock her to sleep.

It is there in our teenagers, going around in bunches, confirming identity with their peers according to their values and beliefs, much of the time to escape the stigma of loneliness, which marks them as "different." It is easy to empathize with those who don't fit in. You may stumble over them in the street gangs where they have escaped to fight for the right to belong to something— anything—that elevates their status to a higher level in society.

And there are old men and women who are left to die behind locked doors in communities that are strange and frighteningly lonely. First Ray, then Bill, and now Judge Richard have all finally given up that ghost of a forgotten lifetime before I have a chance to go back once more to visit them. They probably would not have recognized me anyway.

The silence of loneliness becomes an earth-shattering roar as terror crashes through our complacency. In one flash moment, thousands of lives are lost, some of which have barely begun, and we mourn and cry on in loneliness.

Communities crumble, and the rest of us tremble as we engage in unnecessary war to supposedly rout out terror, offering benevolent promises to restructure nations that have no intention of living peacefully with their holier-than-thou neighbors in the name of Allah, an impossible task for well-meaning nations when years of religious combat have trampled holiness into the hot desert sands forever. Whose side are we on? Who's on our side? Who's on third? Will we ever get to first base in this stupid game of war, losing the youth of our own country in what could be called a handful of soul for a barrelful of oil?

The loneliness I hear around the world comes close enough to touch in solitude now that I am old and no longer lively. But when I think about the children of Haiti, the victims of the China tragedy, the random sufferings of lonely people in need, I cry foul and wonder if I shall live long enough to see them, too, smile.

CHAPTER X

SKELETONS IN THE CLOSET

In this world nothing can be said to be certain, except death and taxes.

Ben Franklin penned those lines back in 1789. I have learned to live somewhat in harmony with the certainty of taxes. But death has had no part in living since Cain slew Abel.

Until recent years we have shoved death into the closet with the family skeletons, never to see the light of day. We have heard the rattle of its bones, but we were afraid to open the door and stare it in the face.

It is difficult to speak of death, for no one can do so with the authority of experience, but the poets, the philosophers, and the theologians have agonized with the essence of it, trying to find the mystery of life in death.

Only in recent history has the fear of death and dying been recognized as a detriment to fully living the here and now.

Breathing in the solace of infinity and rebirth.

The French philosopher Camus in his book *The Fall* writes, "Have you noticed that death alone awakes our feelings?" Khalil Gibran says, "You would know the secret of death? But how shall you find it unless you seek it in the heart of life?" And then, as Robert Graves writes, "We should take our delight in momentariness. In the joy of loving and living, day by day."

I have never forgotten my son Dan's first encounter with death. It was June 6, his birthday, and he was eager to test his skills with his present: a child's bow and arrows. He and his friends raced up into the hills of Makoshika Park whose boundary was across the street from where we lived in Glendive, Montana. He was determined that each one of them would "get a rabbit" for dinner.

A short while later, he was racing back home with the speed of the rabbit he cradled in his arms, hollering, "Give me a hunk a lettuce, Mom, quick!"

I took a look at the limp body in his arms and saw that my son was stifling his breath and sobbing, and I was myself fighting back tears.

"It's too late for lettuce now, son" I told him. "He's not hurting any more, and it's OK to cry, love," I said, hugging him close. I had felt the heartache and the pangs of torment for a life that is lost.

But the whole process of creation points up the reality of a continuing cycle of eternal life, and columnist Kilpatrick says it so beautifully when talking about the resurrection of Easter.

He writes, "Long before there was a Christian faith as such the humblest peasant recognized divinity in April. That which was dead, or so it must have seemed, had come to life again. The stiff branch supple, the brown earth green. This was a miracle. There is indeed, no death. There is indeed, eternal life.

Look to the rue anemone, if you will, or the pea patch or to the stubborn weed that thrusts its shoulders through a city street.

This is how it was, is now, and ever shall be, world without end.

April is remembering, Easter is knowing, and in the serene certainty of spring recurring, who can fear the distant fall.

Who, indeed, should be afraid of death? We should be opening the closet door, however timidly, and inviting the skeletons of death out to dance at the wedding of life."

The gifted Mr. Kilpatrick is no longer with us, but he leaves the thought that the common denominator of a fruitful life is to "hold infinity in the palm of your hand."

As I write in these hours of solitude, Mother, I am remembering you the day we waited with family members and good neighbors for the ceremony to begin.

Members of Penketh Tannery Prize-Winning Band had already stopped by to pay their respects with a rendition of "As We Walk in the Garden" and a cup of your freshly brewed tea before they left.

Remember, Mother, that's when you moved your chair closer to mine as the rest of our company were filing out to the cars behind the hearse where Father lay waiting. Your hand was ice-cold, and your voice trembling as it whispered, "I can't go, luv. I just cannot go. Don't let them make me go. I'll be all right if you will just stay here with me our I."

I would never have left you alone, Mother, and wanted so desperately to comfort you with those words of hope that have long lived after you.

Remember them, Mother? "'Twill be all right come mornin', luv."

"All I desire of my own funeral is not to be buried alive." Chesterfield was a wise man.

CHAPER XI

JUDGEMENT DAY

If I blunder, everyone can notice it.
Not so, if I lie.

There were many tales whirling around in the dust storms of Roswell, New Mexico, when my husband was stationed at the Air Force Base in the early forties. When the dust settled and stars were twinkling in a darkening sky, heaven and earth became one. I was at home there, and the stars belonged to me.

Other folks were out there on their doorsteps, not to gaze at stars, but to wonder what new tales of unidentified flying objects might be tossed around with the winds, spooking people with fears of creatures from another planet that may be snooping around their back yards.

Actually my mind was set on things more down to earth during those days. I was studying to become a bona fide citizen of this beautiful land, America.

I had reached the point of confidence, knew everything I needed to know, and arrived at the courthouse building in Roswell, County of Chavez, State of New Mexico, to become a citizen of the United States of America.

The witnesses who had promised to swear I would make a good American citizen had been closeted with the examiner already when I was called in to stand in judgment alone, more nervous than when I was eating dinner with Lord Leverhulme. My excitement must have been visible to the Fifth Judicial District judge, but the interrogation went smoothly enough, and I was sure that I had it made. The judge smiled and said in his quiet voice, "Just a couple of personal questions now that shouldn't take long."

The questions seemed inconsequential enough. He asked how long I had known one of my witnesses and the frequency of times I had seen him over several years, and had there been any periods of time when I had not seen him. I had answered such a general question without pause or thought, and the judge, with a quizzical look, said, "Have you not traveled abroad in the last three years?" Oh, dear! My dream is about to become a nightmare. I had been exhilarated. I was hearing my father singing, "When it's springtime in the Rockies, in the Rockies far away." I had shot out an answer to a trivial question without first counting on my fingers, forgetting all about the most recent trip home to have Mother meet my first child. It had sounded so trivial that I said, "Yes, sir. I visited England earlier this year."

The judge gave me another look and still with a quiet voice said, "Then you could not possibly have been abroad and at the same time seeing your witness here in the USA during those same weeks as you previously stated, could you? I must ask you to go sit in the waiting area, and I shall call you back in when I have talked again to that witness."

Oh, no! I was waking from a bad dream. I was in shock. I lied in court. How in God's name had my mind wandered away from the business at hand?

What on earth would my witness think of me when the judge questions the truth of his answer to the question of contacts with me?

I was summoned back into the courtroom, given a lecture by His Honor on true statement of fact, and all's well that ends well with a flag of my new country being presented by the judge with a smile and a handshake. I never owned a Union Jack, the flag of my motherland.

Had I earned the right to be honored as a US citizen?

I look today at my serious countenance pictured on this slip of paper, my treasured certificate of citizenship, and I ask myself, "Have you earned the right to be called an American citizen?" I can only truly say I have tried, especially for the rights of women. I have many true and honest witnesses who would gladly vouch for that.

Years later, in Montana, I was asked to speak to the Masonic Lodge members and their wives about America and freedom. It was the Fourth of July, and I dared to test my right to freedom by breaking one of the auxiliary lodge rules that women members must wear skirts. They were not allowed to wear pants at a Masonic occasion.

I tried to look nonchalant walking in line during the opening ceremony, my long, black velvet pant legs making their own notorious statement among short skirts, which shrunk even shorter when their wearers sat unceremoniously, forgetting to cross their ankles and pull their skirts down over their knees. I never did understand that tradition, but it was probably a masculine decision to remind auxiliary wives that men were made to wear the pants.

I was so proud, that night, not merely because of the standing ovation for my belief in our great country. Not one gentleman there on that special Fourth of July celebration spoke out against my beautiful, long black pants. I have kept that symbol of my freedom closeted for sixty-five years.

But I must go back to the seas again, to the lonely seas and the sky, where the wind blows and the birds cry and the tall ships sailing ...

A cabin I will build there of sticks and wattles made ...

I have lived long, but the longing in that poet's voice I will carry with me forever, even though I can never remember his name. There's a tale or two to be told and reckoned with there!

CHAPTER XII

THE INSIDE OUT ABOUT HALLUCINATIONS

To talk of disease is a
sort of Arabian Nights entertainment.
—Osler

This horror story is about a condition called hallucinating, which was caused by one of my medications not agreeing with another, and I knew something was wrong. Very, very wrong. I had become another player on Shakespeare's stage.

In the first place, I didn't *start* this long-playing, ugly scenario, nor was I the leading lady. Neither did I feel exactly like who I was supposed to be: widowed for eight years, grandmother to children I love dearly, an nonagenarian at ninety-two years old with enough courage and gumption to let the whole world read all about the ups and downs of it in a book. Nor was it the booming firecrackers on that Fourth of July celebration a few years ago.

I distinctly remember that particular evening gazing out on a perfectly manicured lawn, the new dogwood tree breathing gracefully beside the red latticed fence, the roses and hydrangeas that Darlene had planted just yesterday making themselves at home under the glorious canopy of my ancient Japanese maple, when the sound of voices drifted over from the far corner of the fence.

A man and woman, with several children scattered across the lawn, were brazenly arguing the difficult task of hoisting a huge, white box over the fence—my fence—and into my good neighbor's garden, a seemingly impossible task to begin with from the look of things.

I immediately took them to task and asked them to *please* leave the premises, but it was like talking to deadwood, and they continued the harangue, the woman brazenly opening a gate, which appeared like magic for their convenience, but definitely not a custom-made gate to fit the immediate transfer of what lay waiting inside the box.

The two put their heads together, screaming as if they were on a deadline to death. Next thing I saw, the woman was pointing up in the tree. Well, you all know how much I love that tree, as if it were a part of me, but there was the man deliberately sawing off its limbs and throwing them down to the woman below who was building something that looked very much like a catapult. By this time, all of the children had climbed up into the empty spaces around the tree trunk, and I didn't want to be sued for accidental fallouts, so I called the police, who didn't respond quickly enough to soothe my ruffled feathers.

Miraculously, then, son Dan entered the scene, assuring me the tree had all its limbs attached, no bodies were flying through the air, and that I should get ready for bed. They tell me it all happened on July Fourth and that it would be all right in the morning, as you, Mother, would soothe your four daughters when calamity struck.

But it wasn't all right in the morning.

The play continued. I was on my way to a gathering of English friends who call themselves the Teasippers. I was the first to arrive and found myself sitting in a chair in the center of a cavernous room, empty except for mummy-like crevices sculpted into the wall, each filled with a live person wearing strange garments.

For instance, the most prominent of them all was moving slowly towards my chair, a specter all deathly pink, square head, no hair, staring eyes giving off an unctuous glare, arms outstretched as on a crucifix, with a pink shroud draped from the wrists to the lower part of his body which was squeezed down to an arrow-point and stuffed into my tall, narrow glass vase that usually stood in a corner of the living room containing an arrangement of poppies and grass. His lips were moving deliberately, but no sound could be heard, even when he stood, hovering over me and mouthing words I could not, or would not, decipher. I knew I was prisoner in this strange room with this extraordinary group of people.

One after another they came to the chair, tormenting me. I begged them to please speak up, but they turned a deaf ear to my pleas. I concluded they couldn't be angelic to hold me prisoner and not allow me the courtesy of *hearing their voices*, so I started throwing out Biblical quotes, in a wild guess they would be acceptable answers to the silent questioning of this maddening crowd.

The strain was becoming unbearable, when I heard friendly voices, Corinne's and Jane's, chastising my tormentors from behind my chair. "Leave her alone; let her go. She doesn't deserve this. Poor Irene!"

At that point a woman in white with a kindly, angelic face glided up to my chair, looked at me sympathetically, and wafted away again.

I don't know how many hours I spent from then on examining the walls, now in my own home, which were disfigured with gray tape and putty and slapped-up ugly paper with maps scrawled all over it, but I found myself eventually standing outside, the pink guy blocking my way from entering my own home. I begged to get inside for my cane, since I was standing, arms full of books, and losing my balance. He was adamant as ever, and I had had it

I was giving him a lengthy sermon about his unholy attitude, which was definitely not good Samaritanism, when a car drove up in the courtyard area surrounding the house. I hollered to the driver for a ride home, but he merely stepped out of the car and stood beside it, like a sentinel.

This phase of the delirium seemed to last forever, with twenty or more black cars coming to a stop in the courtyard; the drivers, all dressed in black, standing to attention by their vehicles as though to cut off my escape from something not quite there. Not one of them made a move to come to my rescue.

From then on, everything was a muddled up mess, with people shouting and pushing through a crowd that had gathered around my doorway.

And then I heard my son's voice, and felt him take my arm, giving me balance once more. Everyone else had disappeared. And he simply told me, "It's past your bedtime. It's four o'clock in the morning. Here's your daily paper. Now, let's get you in and to bed."

He relayed to me later that the *Gazette Times* delivery lady had found me rambling around incoherently outside in the driveway and had tracked down my son who lives close by. His presence brought me down to earth, almost.

I didn't quite feel like myself through that nightmarish time, and I sincerely hope it wasn't catching. But Mother's words got me through the night, and I was right as rain come morning.

My whole purpose since has been to chronicle what I remember and read it to my Friday morning writing group at the Senior Center, hoping to clear my mind of it for good and all and not be accused of writing ipso facto as the experience fades.

My grandson sent me a message, so they tell me, asking why I hadn't written, and I sent him the reply, "I've been busy hallucinating." Surely I must have been of sound mind to be that funny? Let's hope so, Mother.

Now you all know me inside as well as out. And I hope you never experience anything in your life that comes close to it.

I can tell you this much, I would have welcomed Timothy Leary into my life had I known him then. He might have explained to me why everything I attempted to touch during this nightmarish spell immediately crumbled to dust or drifted away from my reach. And, too, if he were involved in any way the whole incident, as far as I have heard, would have been a much more pleasant encounter as in the '40s when people went on "trips" by deliberately ingesting LSD.

Chapter XIII

FRIDAY MORNING WRITING CLASS

If you can speak what you will never hear,
If you can write whatever you will never read,
You have done rare things.

Those words of Thoreau sound almost like a challenge to me. They have carried me through a speaking and writing career that has enriched my life in many ways, especially through the years of senescence.

In the passing of my time, I have overcome fears of speaking on my feet behind a lectern to the point of addressing an audience and feeling the power of knowing my message is reverberating back and forth without a spoken word from those who are listening face-to-face as I speak.

There are many associations out there to help combat the fear of facing an audience and thinking on your feet. My first speech at International Toastmistress Association came out with not much aplomb, so to speak, but with knees wobbling, hands shaking on the speech cards, and hoping the floor would open up so I could hide in the cellar. Yet I persevered long enough to merit winning local, council, and regional contests to compete in the international contest, and to meet women from all members of the organization from around the world.

Toastmasters eventually opened its doors to women, and I took advantage of that opportunity to enjoy doing what I love most: "rare things."

But there is nothing in the world so stimulating as Simon Johnson's Writing Class, especially when your ninety-first birthday is coming up and you need cheering up while recuperating from yet another fall.

Thank God it's Friday today, but what on earth can I write for class. Nothing seems appropriate or worthy of making an effort with umpteen stitches holding the forehead from falling into the eye. I really should stay in bed after the fall the other day.

It usually takes two envelopes of quick-rising yeast for me to raise a toast of praise to anyone, but today I must jump to my feet for it is Simon's birthday, and I promised my classmates I would write something to honor him for the many moons he has devoted to reading between the lines of our weekly efforts.

Several of our members have accomplished the arduous task of finding publishers through the years before the magic of home publishing was made a last-chance gulch. And that spurs us on to success.

I am one elderly widow who looks forward to every Friday in the weeks ahead to "Simon's Scintillating Seminar," the original name bestowed on the class by Dr. John Hult, upon his and wife Adeline's initiation into the group in 1992. They both are published and are now writing conjointly a book based on their amazing lives as missionaries overseas.

You don't hear many octogenarians using the particular abbreviation TGIF (Thank God It's Friday), but you wouldn't believe how many of our sedate senior citizens offer up that benediction, if only in a whisper. I offer it with a sigh and an old woman's wink at God for encouraging me to keep going.

But you definitely have to look where you are going while walking in a parking lot. I still don't know how I made the effort, but there I was in my favorite company, jumping to my feet as I raised the paper coffee cup, with all eyes on my black and blue bruises.

"I raise this toast to honor a man to whom we listen with all our ears, eyes, and inner beings *every* Friday morning.

"Yes, his name is Simon. Not Simon Legree, not the Simon who wrote, 'Cease being the slave of a party and you become its deserter.' And definitely not Simple Simon.

"This devoted Simon is our very own personal professor, Simon Johnson.

"We honor him on his birthday for what he has given to us throughout umpteen years, wholeheartedly and prompt to the minute unless he's taking a well-earned time out paddling his kayak upstream to faraway places, some of which we have never heard.

"Each in our own way we have benefited from his unbelievable knowledge in all things great and small about which we have written and about *how* we have written them. I would even bet that if Merriam and Webster met this particular Simon without hesitation would bind him up in leather and gold leaf and give him a prominent place on the book shelves of history.

'I certainly hope that never happens, because there is so much more about him than mere words can ever describe. For many years he has led this class and shared his knowledge and wisdom with good heart and good sense. We old-timers may take a holiday now and then, but we always come back to play musical chairs for the honor of sitting beside him."

Fellow members delight in each other's company and welcome all newcomers no matter what or how well they write. There's a wonderful feeling of camaraderie and koinonia up, down, and around this table.

The delightful game of Simon Says goes on! And on and on! And by the time two hours slip by, I believe that when I die I shall go on to higher education, hoping Simon will be up or done there.

We celebrate his birthday once a year to honor his being among us and to gift him for the time he spends so freely, sharing his tutorial expertise, his charm, courtesy, and above all, his irresistible sense of humor. When Simon laughs, the whole world laughs with him.

I wish I knew enough about his normal life to give him a real roasting, but let me give you a personal example of how he handles a difficult situation and comes out smiling every time.

A couple of years ago, I caught up with him as he was leaving the class, and I dared ask him, "Simon, do you think the work I present to the class has any chance of being published by a house of good repute?" Well, you can always tell when Simon is thinking, especially on something that's really important to you. That particular Friday morning, he thought for a couple or three seconds and hesitatingly, so he wouldn't hurt my feelings, he said, "Well, I really don't know. It's a harsh world out there you know, Irene, but I'll give it some thought."

I have always respected his direct and honest response to our questions, but this time his thoughts were stretching further than elastic can possibly go. So I kept sitting on the fence while keeping an ear to the ground to even get a whisper from Simon, and I was forced to say to myself, "Don't just sit there—do something."

Well, I won't take time to fill in the details, but when I gave Simon a signed copy of my book, he sent back an e-mail that still puts a smile on my face. He wrote: "Irene, I've read your book, and I'm still thinking on it ... was that an aphorism or something? Simon."

Along with this birthday present to you, which includes our heartfelt thanks, I would like to share a reminder of a day some fourteen years ago, Simon, when you were feted with a poem as being the Wheaties Champion of the Day. We're treating you to Chinese this time, which should taste a little better than Wheaties. But here's the beautiful poem written by Adeline Hult, one who is also here with us today, along with her husband John, who has some of the fisherman's knack of telling a tale. He writes with a humorous twist and is responsible for coining the first name of our close-knit gathering back in 1993.

OUR CHAMPION
At the senior center on Friday morn
Some read serious, some read corn
It's Simon's Creative Writing Class
No tests, no grades, we just don't pass
Simon arrives just on time
In all kinds of weather, rain or shine,
Bu when there's snow on the ground
Be aware ... He won't come around
We write novels with plots so deep,
Or essays which put some of us to sleep;
Our life stories, funny or sad,
And poetry —both good and bad!
He listens to all without exception
Only our worst mistakes does he mention
Too much detail; or it needs expansion
In describing that great old mansion
Simon listens with attentive ear
And so does the class, Oh dear, oh dear!
That perfect story I wrote last night

Was picked to pieces, no hope in sight
Repetition of words gets in my way
And that dance I described was wondrously gay.
Dangling participles or misplaced subject,
But we're here to learn, we don't object
To Simon goes our heartfelt thanks
Tops among teachers he does rank.
Among volunteers Simon stands tall
He's the Champion of them all.
So, thank you Simon from your whole class
We appreciate all that you do for us
—Adeline Hult, 1993 (seventeen years ago and it is still going strong)

Today, in 2011, we are a larger group, even more faithful to our cause than ever, Simon's dedication still spurring us on.

I don't know if the TGIF custom is living still, where employees celebrate each coming weekend with the phrase "Thank God It's Friday," on their way to the nearest pub for a beer and a shot at the poker machines, but our members will sometimes use that phrase in a whisper when Friday comes rolling around.

The pub-goers can have all the beer they can guzzle on those weekly celebrations in the name of freedom. We find our pleasure sipping from spring water bottles or Senior Center paper cups of coffee while sharing the arts and crafts of the written word, with quite a few of our members finding editors who put our words into print.

CHAPTER XIV

A MERRY HEART
DOETH GOOD

They say, "Laugh and the world laughs with you. Cry and you cry alone."

That is definitely not what the Bible says of laughter. Mother would correct you in a minute. Remember what you would say, luv? You would quote from your favorite book, Mother; I think it was from the Book of Proverbs that offers this honest-to-goodness advice: "A merry heart doeth good, like medicine."

I have taken many doses of that medicine to church with me as a lay speaker.

Let me share, too, the words carved on a brass-plated door within the walls of Chester Cathedral, posted there by the architects who designed that magnificently awesome place of worship close to my hometown in England.

Give me a mind that is not bored
Give me a sense of humor Lord
Give me the grace to see a joke
And pass it on to other folk.

Along with all the ups and downs in life, I've learned at ninety-one that you need to sit and consider if your energy is compatible with your desire and ability to succeed before you surge ahead to enjoy life as it breezes by. That is, if you don't battle with the breeze so that it knocks you over.

Remember what Father used to tell me, Mother? "If you grow up with a kind heart and a sense of humor love, you will live to be a hundred." Well, a kind heart speaks for itself, and I have only nine years to go if I really want to fulfill his predictions. I do hope you are laughing wherever you are now.

There have been some shows of injustice, however, that I could never laugh through but only show a smile of forgiveness and merely tolerate the thought of revenge. The first was early in life when our Eve won a scholarship to go on to secondary education. She had scored the best marks over all the pupils chosen, one from each of the elementary schools in Warrington's school district.

Two years later, I was named the winner, looking forward to all of the benefits that went along with the scholastic honor: sports equipment (hockey sticks, tennis rackets), school uniforms, lunches, etc.

What a thrilling moment that was in my life. But it was short-lived. The school board chairman announced that he was so sorry but only one child per family could earn the right to a free education.

Of course, while Eva was enjoying all those privileges, I was a twelve-year-old valedictorian of Evelyn Street Girls School, compelled to spend two more years there because the law demanded I must be fourteen before I could graduate and "go out into the world, find a job, and help my parents financially in repayment for all they had done for me."

Actually, Mother, you were the cause of my delayed overtime in elementary school. You had insisted that I was smart enough to start school when I was four years old!

On that first day away from you, Mother, and the stolid comfort of your very presence in our home, I found myself over and over moving my lips to form your comforting phrase, "'Twill be all right come mornin', luv." It always was and still is.

After elementary school I found a cashier and bookkeeping job in a department store, earning a few shillings a week and keeping out one shilling and sixpence for my own needs. Mother, you saved the rest for a holiday at the Isle of Man where the Manx cats have no tails and the skippers' kippers have too many bones.

Reading textbooks for blind college students was a very rewarding endeavor, filling the mind with history, sociology, philosophy, technical writing, novels by famous authors, and especially that tome of a thousand odd pages of English literature of work back before Chaucer's time and into the present day. How I loved that book. The blind counselor wanted me to reread the book after the tapes had been erased for further use.

All of the books I read were recorded on large machines tailored to enable a blind person to manipulate changing four-track tapes back and forth while listening to their content in order to earn a diploma.

One blind female student wrote a letter thanking me for helping her graduate with honors in English literature.

Gifts like that I shall keep in my heart until the sun and moon go out.

I worked my way around a few legal problems as secretary to a lawyer and much more about education by winning election to a school board position attending to the business of education for ten years. I took advantage of getting college credits by taking courses along with teachers who needed extra credit for a higher position on the salary schedule.

School board trustees in my era often were harassed through the local newspaper, and I remember in our paper one time the *Enterprise* editor wrote of our board members as being a group of unbroken school board puppies who needed to be swatted with a newspaper.

Well our motto had always been to turn a deaf ear, and we kept our dignity by not striking back, but that time we held a heated conference with no one brave enough to volunteer as a spokesman for our displeasure. I was the only woman on the team, so I went home deciding *something just had to be done*.

With a clear mind, I thought up a short retort to hurl back at that enterprising editor then called my married daughter who lived in a neighboring town and asked if she would take a "wanted" ad to our local newspaper.

Of course she would, in her name and at her own expense.

The staff member on duty read the short advert, and controlling his funny bone and with a straight face, pointed Hope to the editor's office, since he knew his head would be blown to smithereens should *he* take the risk of even shoving it under his door.

The editor finally took the handwritten ad, and with as much dignity as he could muster, faced Hope with the expected shock and scorn, "I would never print those caustic words against my character in my own newspaper."

Hope's simple response to the outburst was to remind him of his responsibility to print the news in good taste and without slander and insisted it was his duty to follow the custom of accepting paid want ads for a spot on the right page.

With red face and angry looks, he placed the ad in his in-basket and held out his hand for the cash.

This is what the ad requested.

WANTED
New home for unhappy, unpaid,
UN-HOUSEBROKEN
School District puppies.
PREFERABLY
the lap of an
ebullient efficacious
Enterprising
editor
who has just sold his last
rolled-up newspaper!

Oh, what prevail! Oh, what recompense!

My fellow board members were ecstatic and their confidence restored.

And to this day, no one on that board long ago knew who had written the comeback. My daughter wasn't a local resident and was not a suspect.

I earned a BA degree through life experience and writing a thesis on kinesis to add behind my name in the professional catalogue of the National Speakers Association, earning membership by means of long-time presentations in the International Toastmistress Association, Toastmasters, along with local and area presentations.

I have cherished my citizenship as an American, and, oh, what a wonderful place in which to grow and learn and love. A place where you can laugh or cry as you will without being stuffy about anything, knowing that laughter is the best medicine in the world and costs nothing.

The magic of laughter that lingers with me is when a finger is pointed in my direction, the culprit for something deserving ridicule, I can join in the merrymaking and thus deprive the accuser of expected gratification, and I actually feel the medicine going down.

I can boast of being a Lancashire lass who never dropped her 'aitches like most do, but my funny bone has been tickled over and over again by the healing power of laughter. It has kept me young through the harvest years, and I stop to remind myself of Father's promise, "If you live with a kind heart and a sense of humor, luv, you will live ..."

In the long run, I have learned that a sense of humor can spread a bit of butter when the bread of life goes stale, and we deny the joy in laughter if we are afraid to sing and dance in it—to worship in it!

The mystic Frederic Buchner talked of laughter in an earth-shaking way. He noted that at one time in his life he only went to church because he lived next door to one. He went on to say: "Once, when a famous preacher was relating his message to the coronation of Queen Elizabeth, and Elizabeth, by the way, had a keen sense of humor, I remember she was touring the island of Tonga, a reluctant member of the British Commonwealth, and at one of the events staged in her honor, someone egged her, and the egg spattered all over her beautiful outfit in a very messy manner.

The next morning, as her majesty was addressing the parliament of Tonga, she began, 'While I do enjoy the occasional egg, I much prefer it with my breakfast meal.'

That was a joke. The Queen of England told a joke! Everyone had been on tender-hooks to see how she would deal with the dastardly deed. Off with his head? No. She joked about it. She showed she was human, like everybody else. And diplomatic relations were mended."

I was filling the pulpit in our church (not literally of course) while the pastor was on sick leave, and upon delivering the sermon, I glanced around the congregation to find all eyes open, faces smiling and intent on the message that it wasn't a sin to laugh in church.

And laughter was the best medicine, using that same biblical verse as a message for the Sunday morning sermon, and I might possibly have made a few believers. One of the parishioners sent me the following poem written by Bertha Adams Backus, telling me she was determined to quit feeling sorry for herself so that she could laugh a little more.

Then Laugh
Build for yourself a strong box
Fashion each part with care
When it's strong as your hand can make it
Put all your troubles there
Hide there all thought of your failures
And each bitter cup that you quaff
Lock all your heartaches within it,
Then sit on the lid and laugh
Tell no one else its contents,
Never its secrets reveal
When you've dropped in
Your care and worry,
Keep them forever there;
Hide them from sight so completely
That the world will never dream half;
Then sit on the lid and laugh.

Despite that sound advice, I should warn you that even a well-made, strong box has its own ups and downs, so watch your step!

A CENTENARIAN
AND
A MESSAGE FROM GOD

Her name was Elsie, and the Dial-a-Bus driver introduced her as being one hundred years old as she hoisted herself into the car beside me. She looked much younger than her actual one hundred years and seemed to have a good sense of humor and an excellent memory.

I remarked that I had used a biblical quote in a speech title one time, and before I could say another word, she piped up, "I know the very saying that you chose for a title! It was 'A merry heart doeth good, like medicine,' wasn't it?" She guessed it had been a sermon, so I promised to send her a copy. A few days later, remembering that the employee standing in as a postal clerk at Ace Hardware was not a man of many words and I had never seen him smile, I pushed the envelope toward him on the counter, idly watching him flip it over to read the address on the front saying, "You I answered, yes," relating the story of our meeting and the sermon in the envelope he was holding. He nodded his head with what might have been a smile and asked if I wanted to hear a joke. Without waiting for an answer he began. "A scientist was provoking God into an argument, saying, 'I have some bad news for you, dear God! The wise ones on this good earth have decided that we don't need you any more. We can do anything you can do, sir. You made light; we discovered electricity. You gave us our daily bread; now we make our own manna with the machinery we invented.' And God was silent, suffering throughout the man's prideful boasting, until he hears the words, 'Dear God, we can even reproduce your animals and, listen closely now...'" He stooped to pick up a handful of dust. "'See, we have the stuff to create what you did—a human soul.' And God smiled and simply said, 'Can you *make your own dust?*'" You must admit, He has a keen sense of humor, too.

A SHOT IN THE DARK

My daughter came to visit me over the weekend, and as always we had a lovely time together remembering, looking through old photo albums, laughing at the way things were then, the Panama school hats, the gymslips and the bloomers hugging our knees when I was a schoolgirl.

The sad and the lonely times we have shared were all there, too, as our fingers quickly slipped those pages by to hide our emotion. Lingering a little longer over my wedding album I loved so long ago. I remarked how handsome her father had been.

Hope pushed her chair a little closer to face me across the table. Her eyes, as I looked up at them, held a deliberate dart of curiosity. Elbows on the table, chin resting on the fist she had made with her hands, she said, "Mom, I am going to ask you a very personal question. You might be shocked out of your shoes by my thoughts, but whatever your answer, it will never be repeated to another soul."

Well, I wasn't actually shocked, but the question did pluck a few strings of my heart out of tune when she asked, "Were you ever tempted to cheat on Dad when things became ugly?"

"Who wouldn't?" I countered, my thoughts stalling for precious time to pull together. "That's no answer, Mom! Did you?"

I looked away from her searching eyes, out the window and quickly back again. "Cuppa tea?" I asked. She nodded her head yes, and I busied myself with the teakettle, weighing the pros and cons of self-revelation on such a personal subject as sex, especially extramarital sex. Had I earned the right of passage to share my secret second thoughts on the subject of sacred wedding vows? Would I ever be able to separate myself from the harm inflicted in a wooded lane that was so long pushed into obscurity? Could anyone blame me for dreaming castles in the air? Ought one to fess up to the world such moments of madness when an old woman becomes wearied by the routine drudgery of sex expected at the beck and call of a husband who believed obedience was a wife's obligation and a man's right to demand it?

Such were the thoughts cramping my mind as I dallied over the teapot, stirring the answers round and around with each swish of those things called tea bags. And I wondered, "Do I dare to eat a peach?" Would not my daughter, a young woman of her caliber, be shocked if she thought her father had been betrayed by such a woman? Would I have dared such revelation in a memoir? Maybe I could stretch my truths with fiction, as did the writer of *A Thousand Little Pieces.*

People would forgive me, I'm sure, and put my book on the best-seller list. He stirred up quite a hornet's nest with a little exaggeration.

Still, a memoir is a memoir is a memoir, right?

Author Catherine Bower, tongue in cheek, advises that in writing biography, fact and fiction shouldn't be mixed. And if they are, the fiction parts should be printed in red ink and the fact parts in black ink. Wouldn't that be nice? But as far as I am concerned, the truth of such a tale would be lost between the lines.

I set the cups on the table, thinking of Whitehead's presumption that "Apart from blunt truth our lives sink decadently amid the perfume of hints and suggestions," and I wonder how many memoirists have felt the brunt of that half truth and closed up their laptops for good and all.

I smile a little at the way Nietzsche explains this quandary. He says, "It is good to express a matter in two ways simultaneously so as to give it both a right foot and a left. Truth can stand on one leg, to be sure, but with two it can walk and get about."

With that advice to support my stance, I decided to act on the advice of colleague Matt Amano, who a few weeks ago said to me, "You should write fiction, Irene. You must write fiction!" Well here goes the answer to my daughter's question, Matt. Fact or fiction— you be the judge.

So I wrote my answer into a story for Hope, explaining to her that I was on a speaking tour. Topic: humor!

"Feedback from an appreciative audience was heart-warming, to say the least, and at the conclusion of one of the events, I shook a few hands, returned a few hugs, and then spotted a somewhat handsome man approaching with a grin on his face. He said, 'Appreciated your seminar. Loved your humor. Mind if I use a couple of your jokes now and then? I'd love to hear more, too, if you'd dare to stop in at my room for a nightcap on your way up.'

"Now who could resist an invitation with someone who apparently had a very healthy funny bone? I said, 'OK,' and in no time at all, found myself with a tumbler of sherry in hand. Tasted like Sandeman's actually. Very good. In fact, I asked for another before I should and enjoyed his company immensely. I sipped the wine slowly, lulled by the music of his voice, and counted the strikes of a clock somewhere in the building. Feeling somewhat fuzzy, I rose to say goodnight, but he was already nodding off in his chair, balding head shining under the ceiling light as if he had polished it with O-Cedar.

"Looking on the funny side of things though, if anything else had been expected, it was out of the question, even though some believe that old-timers in this day and age might try anything while there's still time.

Who knows! We may run into each other again in some far off place one day. I'll just take him home with me for a spot of Mother's perfect cuppa tea and a crumpet."

THE UPS AND DOWNS OF A LONG LIFE

Everyone is perfectly willing to learn from unpleasant experience if only the damage of
the first lesson could be repaired.
—Lichtenberg

Those words are just one man's experience, as far as I know, and I prefer to come to my own conclusions in those easy come, easy go upsets in the last stand of a life well lived. I am becoming a pro in the art of falling, because of my failing eyesight and cracks in the sidewalks, but more importantly I have learned to forgive both insult and injury as time flies by.

"Be careful now! Watch your step!" I've heard that warning so often through my life, and it is sound advice for men and women of all ages: a rambunctious child racing around the potted palms in the theatre foyer, an older sister trying out her first high-heeled shoes on the slippery kitchen floor, and someone who should have known better than expect to get up on a bicycle while suffering from vestibular imbalance.

Falling is a particular hindrance to the elders, especially if, as the poet suggests, you "wear purple with a red hat that doesn't go." To which I add: "... but match my failing green eyes that are squinting at the computer screen too long at a time and can't see much beyond my nose."

The only grudge I bear about my latest fall is that my walking stick lost its head as it flew out of my clutches. But actually I kept my head and composure all the way through a profusely bleeding gash over one eye, a few bruises, and a brain concussion that was of no consequence according to my daughter-in-law, the radiologist, who reported to me, "Nothing to worry about, Irene. Your brain is the size of a sixty-year-old's." I was really stunned when she called back later to apologize for her report. The brain scan was given a second reading by a co-worker who reported that he viewed the brain as being even twenty years younger than sixty! I still think they were both puling my leg.

After the whole dreamlike experience of an ambulance ride to the hospital emergency facility and getting the stitches above my eye, the remainder of the day I was able to accept and handle what was once the fear of falling. I had been an avid reader in earlier years and had studied an experiment by Dr. Viktor Frankl, a psychiatrist who had developed a clinical approach to overcoming fear. It is called "paradoxical intention" and can easily be found on the Internet.

SINGIN' IN THE RAIN

My life alert system was the saving grace in this fall, but the way I landed was by no means a ballet performance.

Twisting and groaning, I managed to turn over and sit up with the help of my cane, which I then used as an SOS, waving it in circles through the air, hoping somebody, anybody, would see a damsel in distress and run to the rescue.

Nobody came, no doors were opened, no cars turned left from the avenue into our Chinaberry Place. I was helpless, sitting in a puddle of water, waving my trusty walking stick at nobody in particular and singing to myself Mother's little ditty, "Pack All Your Troubles in Your Old Kit Bag," and smile, smile, smile, Prince Charming came galloping around the corner in his postal vehicle and spotted my cane waving at him from across the street.

He was over to my side in a flash, saying he wasn't allowed to pick me up, but he kindly put his jacket over my shoulders and his driving gloves on my cold, wet hands.

He noticed the Life Alert button hanging from a lace around my neck, and I told him it would only operate around the house and a few yards away from it, as I had understood when signing up for that emergency device.

He asked me to take it off, took a look at the printing on the back, and found a telephone number. Off to locate a phone, he came back within a few minutes with good news that help was already on its way. The fire engine was soon screaming its way around the bend, and four handsome, young men were lifting me to my feet in one fell swoop.

Today a young lady came to install a brand-new system for my use, and when I mentioned this recent fall and thanked her for the company's good service, telling her how the postman had used the phone number on the back of my alert button since the devise would kick in no more than a few yards away from the house, she gasped and said, "Oh, no! Just picture the length of a football field as the number of yards your Life Alert button will summon help for you when you need it. We are always happy to watch over you, but do take care to watch your step."

FALLING OFF THE CITY BUS

I fell off the city bus one rainy day. The driver forgot to warn me to "watch your step now," and at the same time did not fully lower his bus steps enough for me to even reach the ground or see it either, since I was loaded down with Christmas gifts, a sneaky umbrella that had a habit of springing open unexpectedly, my trusty cane, and the kind of large, bulky handbag all sensible lady shoppers would never leave at home.

Too late the bus driver left his seat to find me flat on my back on rough paving strewn with the makings of a Merry Christmas. He attempted to pull me up by the hands, a futile attempt, since he was by no means a muscle man.

He shouted, "I'm going to call an ambulance!"

"Don't you dare. I'll refuse to go! I am not hurt." And a little more assertively, "I'll just roll over onto my knees and get up by myself, thank you very much."

Doing so on hard paving was a painful process and so humiliating knowing that the bus had stopped outside of Starbucks where the customers would have a good view of that unladylike behavior.

There wasn't the slightest premonition that I would herald the next year's Christmas morning with a bigger bang.

THE CHAIR THAT WASN'T THERE

Christmas had rolled around again, and everyone was agog. My son Dan's home up the hill from my house was the gathering place, and daughter Hope had said she would telephone me the next morning before she came down to pick me up.

Well, I was eighty-seven years old at that time and decided that after a late-night Christmas Eve I deserved to sleep in a little later than usual. But no! Before I had closed my eyes again, there goes the telephone ringing in my computer room.

Many people feel obligated to hurry to answer a ringing telephone in case it is an emergency call, and I am no exception.

I reached the computer room chair, which was within reach of the telephone, and it all happened in a flash, because I had forgotten there was a long, slick mat for my cozy chair to slide along, with me in it, to get where I wanted to go in a hurry.

I quickly found that as you grow older, you slow down, especially under such circumstances, but it could have been the rum in the Christmas pudding. I started to leave the chair to rise to my feet and pick up the phone, but the chair decided to go skating backward from under me, and I fell flat on my back on the mat.

I don't know how long I lay there, but my brain did start to work. I decided I wouldn't be able to get up alone to unlock the door for Hope to come in, but I did try to sit up and succeeded in spite of the pain.

"Now, how does one travel the length of this house?" I moaned, trying to twist my body around. As I did so, I was able to slide inch by inch on my bum to reach the front door, hoist myself up on the shelves of the bookcase there, and with a long breath of relief, unlocked the door and found my way slowly back down to the floor.

Leslie, my daughter-in-law, is an MD and had come down with Hope, thinking she might be needed, as I hadn't answered Hope's call.

In her usual pleasant voice, she gave me a quick look over saying, "Irene, I'm going to take you down to the emergency center. I believe you have broken your back."

Christmas day was definitely not a time to be in a hospital, and how could I possibly spoil that wonderful holiday for all my loved ones? So I persuaded them to make the couch comfy next to the dining room table, and I would still enjoy the celebration of the year.

The verdict the next day was that I would go through a new surgical procedure for broken bones, but my turn to await this new venture could be two more weeks.

The surgeon would insert through the skin on my back a needle full of a substance that would cement the separated vertebrae back together again.

COME ON DOWN!

'Twas a dark and dreary night as we were cautiously walking with the crowd down the middle of the street, even though my daughter-in-law Leslie had her arm tucked into mine to help me navigate the throng weaving a one-way course, with heavy hearts I might add, to the same destination, far, far removed from Oregon State University's Gill Coliseum. The last game of the men's basketball season had bit the dust, and our young heroes had given up the ghost at the final buzzer. Oh what price glory! It shone from the eyes of the opposing team.

A cold wind was bearing down on us, and I seemed to be dawdling, so son Dan took my other arm, and with cane clutched in my hands, I was almost flying on a horizontal course until we finally reached the parking lot.

Rounding the bend in the road, my eyes focused on an SUV, which must be our vehicle. I asked Leslie, "Are we there?"

"Yes, turn on your lights, Dan." Dan let go of my arm and stepped ahead of me to flick on his lights, as I naturally thought to help me up into my side of our heavenly high vehicle, when my lights dawned.

The light was shining from the vehicle parked just ahead of the SUV I thought belonged to us.

I really didn't begrudge walking a step or two further past the unlit shape to my left, to be sure of a comfortable ride home, but suddenly, lo and behold, that unlit son-of-a-gun was backing up on me and would have run over me had not Leslie screamed, "Watch out, Irene," while banging with all her might on the SUV that wasn't ours.

I backed up, fell on my back, and all I remembered afterward was a license plate with letters seeming to read: COME ON DOWN.

They say an accident like that happens in a split second, and when my son called to check my condition the next morning, I said, "It's amazing how your mind races as you are falling," and I proceeded to impress him with how I reacted in that split second between heaven and earth.

"*Ipso facto*, Mother. You are making conclusions from the very nature of the case." "Ipso facto to you, too, my dear," I said to myself. Those fleeting thoughts, rather, are an assertion made but not proven. *Ipse dixit*, if you please. He hung up as soon as he was assured that I was in my right mind. He didn't remember that I once worked for a lawyer.

I am still going to finish this ramble in the dark and share my thoughts and feelings of that so-called split-second ipso facto with my present company, a group of caring, understanding fellow writers.

You may make your own conclusions between ipso facto and ipse dixit, but if you are like me, you probably will want to forget all about a tale that has not rhyme nor season but is definitely within reason.

I think Albert Camus would agree that falling is no fallacy. It is real and horrifying for anyone to end up in that kind of ungainly position. But what if the mind is alive to the danger of the situation and races on in that short period between life and possible death, to guide me with a warning of danger that stopped me in my tracks parallel to that oncoming license plate. And as I tried to turn around to speed out of harm's way, I started to fall backwards instead. Instantly came the image of a collision with fate leaving me flat on the ground not breathing.

But my mind responded, "Do something, and be quick about it!" In that small space of time falling, I remembered my broken back in a fall from the year before.

The internal dialogue played out. "Which side of your back?"

"The left!"

"OK. Turn your body to the right, stupid." I swear I inclined my body purposely to guide its direction, thus avoiding damage to that portion of my spine once again.

As my head hit the ground, all the porch lights in the world were spotlighted on my dilemma, deliberately focusing on the *words*, now spelling out my obituary engraved on that piece of metal called a license plate. I swear it read: COME ON DOWN!

Well, I wasn't ready for that kind of injustice, so I dug in heels and elbows, trying to push my body backwards out of harm's way and losing my shoe in the bargain. Dan was by my side asking, "Did you break anything?" And when I whispered, "I don't think so," he circled his arms around my waist, trying to lift me in a full nelson, which actually would have taken Lord Nelson's full crew to accomplish. All the while, Leslie was instructing him, "Don't do that. Don't do that," fearing that I *was* all broken up.

The porch lights dimmed, and my flickering lights followed suit, for I don't remember how they hoisted me to my feet and into the high-rise vehicle again, still thinking of that message from hell on the license plate, I said, "I'd rather you take me home than go out to dinner with you, if you don't mind."

They showed their sympathy. Leslie told me to take a Tylenol, but minutes later I was saying to myself, "Go. Quit feeling sorry for yourself. It'll be all right come morning." I ate my share of sweet and sour at the Thai place along with a glass of their excellent beer. The world was round again. I slept and woke with only a skinned elbow and a bruised ego.

THE HEAVENS FALL
AND
ALL HELL BREAKS LOOSE
Permission to Rise From a Fall
With Dante

I woke this morning wondering if my brand-new furnace, installed but a fortnight ago, had slipped a switch or two and was running rampant through the night. No, it was quite cool outside the sheets. I rose, checked the thermostat, still sixty-eight degrees, so I decided I might as well start the day at the old computer, working up another sweat, trying to remember whatever had given me such a hot flash in the first place.

And as my fingers fumbled for the keys on the keyboard, the screen yawned back into consciousness and I remembered the night before when I had fallen in love with Dante, even though this brilliant author had created his hero Virgil, searching the concentric circles of hell to lay claim on the virgin queen of perfection, Beatrice. I thought that was an enticing scheme to start a story.

All heaven burst loose for me though, and there I was, too, circling the River Styx seven times, in a nightmare chase after Virgil who's only intent was chasing after Beatrice who apparently didn't give a damn *who* was chasing her through hell and high water to stake a claim on her perfect body. Such pomposity. Such a self-seeking bigot she was! But Virgil was dauntless in pursuit of his golden girl and was not at all shaken when his valiant efforts fell short at every turn, where I almost got ahead of him.

I don't remember actually reading beyond the "Inferno" portion of the *Divina Commedia*, but I suppose I will have to in order to find out for myself if it ends up a comedy or if *commedia* is just another one of those ipso facto words buried in a dead language.

However, if memory serves me right, it was the antique scholar Charles Williams taking a square look into this author's theosophy that cleared the whole scene up for me. He pinpoints Dante's thesis in just a few words, and I had to read them twice to dig so deep. He said, "Unless devotion is given to a thing which must prove false in the end, (I always knew she wasn't on the up and up), the thing that is true in the end cannot enter. But the distinction between necessary belief and unnecessary credulity is as necessary as belief itself. It is the heightening and purifying of belief."

I'll believe that next time I'm tempted to climb the clouds to heaven, but it was Dante who wrote this famous book wasn't it? Brains definitely come before beauty in my book! And who can blame me for giving up on poor old Virgil and his dream of perfection. He didn't realize that the sly Beatrice was just pushing on ahead to polish up the apple, which, even then, in Dante's days, had lost its bloom. And I'm a bit too old for games like that, anyway.

I'd swim the river Styx seven times sixty to meet a mind so unencumbered. I don't give a hoot what he might look like. And who knows, he might just show up himself in my dreams tonight!

CHAPTER XV

TAKE ME HOME

One's real life is often the life one does not lead.

Oscar Wilde's aphorism seems to be written especially for my husband, who suffered from Alzheimer's long before that name was understood by most people. He had been diagnosed as schizophrenic, trying to live in a world of misconceptions.

It was a sad day when we moved him, along with his furniture and personal belongings, into a place behind locked doors. When he said, "We'll stay in this hotel overnight, will we, and fly back home tomorrow?" I didn't have the heart to correct him. I just responded, "We'll see," and wondered how many more excuses I would need to dream up and still hold on to that thing called integrity.

I wondered, too, if I could muster the strength to go back there the next day. But I did and again the next day and the day after and after that, until I felt like the mother of all those poor souls in Regent Court.

It was so easy to make friends with people who so desperately need the love and comforting presence of someone who might be there to take them home again. Not to the place they wouldn't recognize when they got there, but to the warm, safe place of belonging they used to know. A rightful place of personage they once had, the selfhood so rudely snatched away from them as they hopelessly reach out in a dark underworld that has slammed the door of understanding in their faces.

The pity is tinged with fear now every time the phone should ring. I gave permission to the nurses for him to call me at any time, and there it goes. I think, "Oh, no. Not again." But yes, it is my husband again, and my heart sinks to a new low. "Irene, come on now. Let's get on the road! We have a long way to travel tonight and not much time to get there."

Where we were going, I didn't ask, and again I used the old cliché about his heart.

He insisted that we owned three houses in town, and since I didn't want him any more, he would take the one that was furnished and was quite capable of taking care of himself. I searched for another bit of logic he might accept for staying where he was until he regained his strength, reminding him of the two heart attacks that had destroyed over half of his heart muscle, but he pooh-poohed that away, so I had to be firm and tell him he wasn't going anywhere with that kind of attitude. "Oh, all right. We'll start packing tomorrow then."

And I wanted to run away. Far, far away where I could hide my face from the world and curl up like a caterpillar to sleep and wake up with beautiful wings.

I know I will be going again tomorrow. We would make clay pots with the rest of his neighborhood, people with the early stages of Alzheimer's, according to his entrance examination. He would sit beside me, rolling his ball of clay into a nothing while I was showing him how a pot should look in different stages of its growth. He would sit for a few more minutes, put his chin on his chest, and go to sleep. The minute he wakes up he asks, "Are we home yet?"

Or we would sit in the makeshift chapel, mostly wheel-chaired rows of pews, listening to a visiting preacher tell us about the good life ahead. I tolerated the sermon because Ray seemed to enjoy the piano and guitar that thumped out the hymn tunes. Then he would tire and go to sleep again whispering, "Take me home."

The rest of the time, we sit on his bed while he begs me to pack up his bag and take him home. Outside on the patio bench, he would hold my hand and beg me to take him home.

I promised to stay until after dinner that day, and we sat in his usual place at a table with two other residents. There wasn't much talking except when Richard, the neighbor across the ward from him, started to choke on a piece of meat and spit it out, along with his teeth, onto the tablecloth. I helped him separate the two, and we somehow got his teeth back inside his mouth again. He looked up at me and said, "I have been very sick, and I love you." This beautiful soul, wheelchair-bound, barely able to hold up his head, had once been a prominent judge, and from my acquaintance with him in that place, I knew his judgment would be upright, honest, and in due consideration for all parties concerned.

That same evening, Alice pushed her walker over from another table to complain that yesterday Frances, her neighbor, had been begging Alice to take care of her because "Nobody else would, and NOBODY comes to see me any more." Alice, being somewhat forthright and opinionated, told her, "No! I have enough to do to take care of myself."

She went on to relate her daily account of how they put her husband in a different home and said, "They won't listen to me when I tell them we should be together."

Frances, on the other hand, thought she deserved the hugs I gave her every day, because she was more than half deaf and said, "People think I'm stupid." When I told her that I had the same problem and if she asked them to "please speak up; I'm deaf," they would understand that she certainly was not stupid but very intelligent.

Bill was a colonel in some battalion or other during World War II and lived across the way from Ray's room in this care facility, with a nameplate on his door, just as my husband had on his door.

This neighbor was sitting at a different table for dinner one night, and later I learned why. Among the residents of all four divisions at the Court, no matter how long they had resided there, Alzheimer's ran rampant, and Ray, who also was suffering through glaucoma, had mistaken Bill's room for his own and was looking around, probably more mixed up than ever with nothing recognizable there.

Bill spotted him and came, fists up in front of his face, charging into Ray's room to challenge the thief who was messing around in his abode. Raised fists from anyone, colonel or no, would raise anybody's gander, and my husband, the sergeant, took the challenge right back to the colonel in the form of a karate kick and an angry order to get out of *my* room! Details were hazy, since the needling facts had been lost in a haystack of pent up emotion.

After the dinner, biding my time until the dreaded third act goodnight scene, I hoped upon my departure this time for just a kiss, my husband being all readied for bed and in a somewhat vacant mood.

Hope went with the wind, however, and my heart sank with the *Titanic* as I saw the colonel coming on like a cyclone trashing everything in his path. Ray shot up from the bed, fists upraised, shouting, "Come into *my* room will you, you s*6^@ b." As I stood between them, warding him off, the colonel's reply was, "Let me at him. I'll take him on any time."

I was hollering for an aide during the standoff, pushing with my hands against two pairs of fists making their mark in all the wrong places, when the aide, one of the young people who volunteered or were paid minimal wages to handle such trauma, arrived to help me disentangle myself, and she finally persuaded the colonel to go for a cup of tea.

The goodnight kiss did nothing to settle Ray down that night, but I had to catch the last bus and knew he would be hurrying behind me as I headed for the outside door, which, of course, was locked for good reason. As usual he tried to remember the numbers I punched on the phone dial that would guarantee his freedom, and I felt the pains of desertion for him, as I did for my father years ago. I make my exit in the two seconds the door gives me to escape his sobbing and pleading to take him home, and I know I have to go back there again tomorrow and the next day and all the days after.

"Wait for me! Please, please, wait for me. I hate it here." He had already tried to climb the high fence with no success and rattled the locked gates until they creaked. I didn't turn around as I made my getaway, so he didn't see my stiff, British upper lip quivering.

It all brings back my dear father lying in a cot outside an English sanatorium where cold air and isolation was the cure for the contagious disease tuberculosis with which he was diagnosed, crying to come home to his girls. He died, shivering and breathing in that cold air of no hope, everyone believing it was for his own good. Then I learned from his death certificate that he had suffered through the horrible pain caused by carcinoma of the lungs through all those lonely days of the T.B. cure! I still wish with all my heart, Mother, that we had known, so we could have brought him home.

I still have his letter to you saying that he wanted to be home with his girls and asking you to bring him another homemade custard pie.

I asked myself many times during Ray's days behind locked doors, "Dare I take him home with me?" I know I will get up and go again tomorrow to Room 104.

I was met by one of the young girls who brightened up the place every day, and she said, "Before you go in to Ray, would you like to hear a funny story?" I nodded my head yes, expecting a quick one-liner, and then I'd be ready to face the day. She went on, "We lost Ray last night." My thoughts went right away to the locked doors, the fence, the locked garden gates, but she shook her head. The four sections of the building were separated by locked doors also, each one identified by a fancy name but actually housing renters in various advanced stages of Alzheimer's.

Ray had a habit of moping around the corridors in the night and would wander through any section door that had been left open. The aide went on, "I alerted the other staff when I was making a routine check after lights out and found him missing. We went in different directions, finding nothing, and came back again to the room to talk things over."

The room was one of two bedrooms that made up an apartment with a shared bathroom dividing them; the other bedroom was not occupied at present but decked out as a showroom for the Alzheimer's caretakers looking for cozy quarters for the loved ones they were letting go.

I asked if they had looked in there.

"That was the very last place we looked," she said. "We were on our way out, and I glanced over the other side, and there he was, sleeping like a baby in that lovely bed. I went over there and shook him awake," she went on, "pulling down the bedclothes. And there he was ... naked as a newborn baby, his clothes all neatly folded on the table beside him. 'Ray,' I said, 'what on earth are you doing here in his bed? This is not your bed!' 'I know it's not my bed,' he said, 'it's my wife's bed, and I have every right to be here.'

"'No,' I said, 'you come back to your own room. It's right over there, and we'll tuck you into your own bed, Ray.' He came quiet as a lamb. I pulled up the covers over him, and he was asleep before I could turn around."

The rest of my time there we spent listening to his favorite '40s songs played by another guest on the piano in another section of the place.

The next day was Sunday, and my daughter, who came to see him every other week, a three-hour drive from where she lives, brought a huge seedless watermelon for him, one of his favorite treats. She set it on the serving counter outside of his room after borrowing a knife from the kitchen, and Alice poked her head out the door of her room. "Ooh, watermelon!" she hollered, and we invited her over to try some.

She was on her second slice when Bill took it for granted that he would be welcome and pulled up a stool. Then Frances and Rebecca (of Sunnybrook Farm she told me), who was so proud of being a Girl Scouts leader for thirty years. Esther brought her baby—her big rag doll—and Ayie, who always invited me to go see her in her beautiful home in Maui. She would chuckle whenever I said, "Hi, Ayie," I see Richard's wheelchair at the other end of the counter. Rachel was invited to the feast by her boyfriend, and when I asked her if she would like a slice, her friend spoke up, "She won't eat it."

"Oh, yes, I will eat it," she snapped and ate three helpings just to show him.

In no time, the hall was crowded. Everyone said they had a good time, and there wasn't an empty plate except for Judge Richard's, who was triumphantly spitting out his teeth with the one pit that I told him wouldn't be there in that seedless watermelon.

Ray's only comment after the party was, "Those old geezers really enjoyed that watermelon, didn't they?"

Esther lost her shoe that day. I spotted her, feeling her way around the walls encompassing the Valley Commons, the place of the First-Stage Alzheimer's patients. She was sliding her two hands along the shiny brass rail that spanned those walls, her feet slowly and cautiously keeping pace like a dancer learning a two-step. A-one-and-two-and-stop-and-rest. A-one-and-two-and-stop-and-rest. A one-and-two … and then the wall outwitted her. It snatched the rail right out of her grasp and took it around a corner. Utterly confused at this turn of events, Esther lost her balance, along with her shoe, and bent down, feeling around the carpet trying to locate it. In the process, she crumpled in a heap on top of it, and I rushed across the room to help her onto her feet. She waved me away with a haughty flip of her hand but then reconsidered and allowed me to feel underneath to retrieve her shoe and slide it onto her foot. Again she refused the hand reaching out to help her up and managed to rise as far as her knees. It was pitiful to see her dignity sinking down into that shoe, and tears were very near the edge as she crawled around still groping for a shoe that was on her foot. She had nothing left but to give up, and she looked me in the eye and said, "I'm going to go to sleep now." And her troubled mind went along with her, until I located an aide to see what the staff of an Alzheimer's community would do in the situation.

I saw Esther shuffling around our room the next day, the rag doll cradled in her arms. I said good morning and asked if I could "see her new baby," and she rewarded me with a smile and proudly turned the doll around for me to see.

I am becoming so fond of these new friends of mine that I'm tempted to take them all home with me.

The facility is a very comfortable, caring place for those who can afford it. They do not accept Medicare, and my bills ranged between three and four thousand dollars a month plus toiletries, bedding, linens, furniture, and as much as eight hundred dollars in prescription medications per month.

Some of the residents in the court seemed to find happiness there, in step with their level of understanding the disease allowed them, in their home away from home that wasn't home. Unless I promised to participate, my husband refused all the activities except rides in the company bus, which possibly offered him a plan of escape.

He especially liked the outings we planned for him and made himself at home trying to help put up my paintings, ready to sell at the art show. What he enjoyed most was just sitting there with a smile on his face, a burger in one hand and a Coors Light in the other. With all the medications included with his diet, alcohol was ordinarily off limits for him, but we thought it would be a nice thing to do just once since it was the other thing that he begged for every day, along with his freedom. We let him think he was getting away with something. When we returned to the caring place that day, he was smiling, and at the front door, he asked, "Is this the bank?"

On another occasion my daughter and I planned a surprise picnic for him in the city park. It was all spread out there before him as a surprise: his children, his grandchildren, the chicken and potato salads, and all his other favorites. Especially the beer. His eighteen-year-old grandson who had flown in from Montana was playing his own compositions on the guitar, and Ray was delightedly sipping up a beer and a little outdoor sunshine.

We reminisced and laughed and ate ourselves sleepy when dusk arrived a little early.

"We'll drive Grandpa back," our eldest son suggested, and I breathed a sigh of relief that I would not be going through the escape routine that night. They told me that when they walked him through the entrance, still smiling, he shouted to all who were close enough to matter, "This is the happiest day in my whole life!"

It was to be the last happiest day of his life.

Pascal says, "Grace is indeed required to turn a man into a saint; and he who doubts this does not know what either a man or a saint is." Mother, I pray my husband is at peace among the saints.

It was a very unhappy time of my life, with neither rhyme nor reason to it, but the only way to get through such misery, I found, was to quit feeling sorry for myself and "walk it off," as you would say, Mother.

I was awakened late the next evening with the words coming out of the phone, "Irene, Ray just died, and we need to know the name of his funeral parlor."

What a stiff, cold message so close to a happy family reunion. What an impersonal way for anyone to relate sad happenings, but, oddly, somehow it seemed to be in context with the way he had lived. Even so, I had lived beside that husband and father of three for sixty-two years and deserved respect for even the slightest iota of bereavement that I might be feeling at his passing. The news of his death came as a stunning blow, robbing me of all conscious emotion as I ran around the house, crying, "No! No! No! Oh, No!"

I had asked the caller to contact my son, who lived close by, and he took over from there. We drove to the Court, and I asked to see my husband. He was stretched out on his back on the bed with his head turned sharply away to the left in a pose of resistance and almost of defiance. When I bent down to touch his face, he was far, far away on his lone island. He wouldn't turn around. He would *not* turn around to recognize me. And I knew he was dead.

God alone can put any measure on the amount of love we give and receive in this life, and God alone will ever know how much of it I tried to give. My only consolation will be to never look back with regret, if I can help it, on whatever I did in good faith.

My eight-year-old grandson sat beside me at the military funeral on September 5, 2001, holding my hand, holding back his tears, with a glance now and then to see if he was behaving like a gentleman.

A salutation of shots was fired in the air by men who had courageously lived through more deadly shots fired in the same "war to end all wars." And the poignant notes of the trumpeter playing "Taps" were still resounding among the tall, stately evergreens guarding the graves in that quiet place. And now the Honor Guard was in formation to fold Old Glory with such dignity and respect for what it meant to have served under that beautiful flag in the same war that my husband had once fought. I had forgotten it would be presented to me, to keep in memory. They asked if I had anything to say, and I assured them I did. Not to those present but to my husband, lying in the coffin ready to be covered with the cold, black earth. I stepped up to the grave and read a letter I had written to you, Ray, and these were the words I know you heard.

"On a September day sixty years ago, I stood beside you, and we said, 'I do,' and so we did. We have stuck together through thick and thin for all those years since that day in 1943, holding the promise of 'til death do us part on this very spot.

"The road may have been rocky in spots and the ice too thin to skate upon, yet I regret not one minute of all those years together. I thank you for the security you provided me as a stranger in a foreign land.

"I thank you for my children and for the principles, though harsh, you expected them to follow; the love for your country; your passion for hard work; your insistence on truth at all costs. They have passed along those virtues to our grandchildren, and I thank you for that. I know that you felt all of our love for you last Sunday at the picnic we shared in Avery Park, and I feel in my heart that you were proud of our children and how they were raising their own.

"We have to learn to accept love as well as to give it. You received all of our love with open arms that day, and I know it helped you find peace. I found comfort and peace myself in that thought soon after your death while driving home in the most beautiful sunset I had ever seen.

"And now I can celebrate your passing, certain that you have given up to an even greater love where there will be many picnics in the park. Your wife, Irene."

Two months later, I stood in my kitchen doorway on a gray November day, looking out at the Japanese maple, my head swaying in rhythm with its bare branches, rejoicing with them in their promised freedom to hang on to their welcome release from endless unneeded crew cuts from the man of my house who didn't know quite what he was doing.

The rain-soaked tree stands black against the lightening clouds, its characteristic white markings wending their way in brazen contrast up and around the bark until they vanish out of sight among the twigs and branches. If sun and rain make peace together next spring, those branches would be laden with leaves, casting their dancing shadows on the deck, and I suppose I would need to do a little trimming myself then.

I breathed a sigh of relief, remembering how that beautiful Japanese maple suffered year after year: harsh pruning that never allowed the tree to reach its full glory.

"It'll grow back," he always insisted. But there was never enough time for full recovery before the sun went down on summer. And even today, with his harsh pruning but a memory, the old survivor stands, holding her breath until spring comes shearing round again.

Chapter XVI

QUIT FEELING SORRY FOR YOURSELF

"Stop to breathe in the view, and the serendipitous, the unexpected, might just reach out and grab you by the heart strings," I say to myself and decide to join a poetry group, people who love words and know how to put them in a nutshell.

I didn't stay long enough to publish even a disc of doggerel, but I did manage to rid myself of a lingering guilt regarding church vows that once bound me to writing a memoir, with a recent attempt at turning it into poetry.

PROMISES UNBROKEN
I was told they should last forever.
And promised at the altar "evermore"
So I swore before God those right Holy words to honor, love and obey.
My cup runs over with pure, golden honey.
But the man of my dreams,
along with the ring,
Then threaded those vows on
a piece of old string
To hang round my neck
at his beck and call
in a brand new scheme of things
The faithful swan, like me, would never cede to such indignity
And not turn tail on her chosen mate

But this ugly duckling swore to keep
those vows of nineteen forty-three.

Such niceties were born and bred in me
So I lost them, purposely, in the field of golden daffodils of which the poet speaks
to this stretched-out spandex world.
I hid them there my promises fluttering with the daffodils
But on one dark and dreary day the lovely flowers died In a shrouded field where
once they danced with glee…
Giving rise for all to see those hidden vows
and the pall they'd cast over me
In retrospect, I scattered seeds of dandelions then,
brazen, unwanted weeds they were,
hundreds of their yellow heads, sprouting overnight it seemed.
In spite of hooves and heels that tracked them down relentlessly,
they rose to bloom again.
Such a cover of deceitful will, to keep my promises unbroken still.
Spoken in earnest, innocent of truth, after so many years
of stifled breath and brittle honey I hear them still,
sotto voce, begging pardon now that he has gone—their executioner.
So I break the old worn ugly string, and set them free
To float on high with dandelion seeds
Seeking other company

But should not I have worn them proud, I ask myself,
As proof of chastity?
A show of strength to save my dignity
Now that I am old, and hold myself accountable

I hear that today age is all the rage, and there is (according to a news article by Hope Yen) an elite club of 340,000 or more centenarians across the world who are leading healthy, happy lives enjoying a game of golf … and I suspect dancing in the dark after a few martinis in the clubhouse, testing out their wings, anything to keep their wits alive as well as their bodies. I would bet my money on a few of those old busybodies being fit enough to challenge Tiger Woods in his heyday off the greens. Those centenarian golfers must already be hitting well under par and putting a hole in one, or *someone* if their sight is failing.

My husband and I used to play at golf, but his ball would always go to the left, and mine would stubbornly swing to the right of the course, giving spectators the idea that "those two old-timers are already separated or headed in the right direction for a divorce!"

In the olden days, you might have heard, "One hundred years old? I don't believe it! What a miracle! How do they do that?" If that marvelous association keeps on going for another ten years, I aim to join them to find out what kind of superglue they use to hold on to life that long.

THE PYURN STORY

Meanwhile, a year or so ago, I planned to modernize this little gray home in the West after a long search to find a contractor whom I decided would have the same sense of perfection, earnestness of purpose, and the goodwill to compromise, all of which I proclaim are my own principles.

I finally found one. Alas, it was just after the memorable day when I fell off my computer chair and broke my back.

Pyburn was the name of the construction company I hired. Rick, his sons, and crew accomplished the job of inserting a door from my bedroom to the lawn with a small deck outdoors to use as an escape hatch in case of emergency.

You can guess my relief as the plaster started to fall from the wall imprisoning me after seventeen years with no escape from fire on that side of the house.

To let the sunshine in, I choose a glass patio-style door, which needed to be covered during the building process to protect my eyes from the sun and nosey neighbors peeking in on their late evening stroll. The only thing large enough in the house to cover that huge pane of glass was a wrinkled, old white sheet, and I watched dejectedly while the workers hung it.

It looked as miserable as I felt lying there on my bed, trying to recover from a broken back.

"Have you ever been lonely? Have you ever been blue?" There is something haunting in those two lines from an old song, but I never seem to have enough time to be lonely, and, besides, I hear me talking to myself quite often these days, and its surprising what I learn when I stop to listen.

I do have many friends, however. In fact they are scattered across the country and some around the globe, thanks to Globe Pequot, publishers of my first book. I also have a close bond with the plumber, the gardener, the mailman, the butcher, the baker, and the candlestick maker. And the Pyburn clan!

They told me they wouldn't leave until the job was done and my door completely settled in, even if it took all night.

Sleep doesn't come easy, however, and the day starts early as I find myself growling, "Good God! Morning already?"

As I turn over to ease my tired bones, I look at my new door, and the words speak out for themselves, "Good morning, God."

The old sheet was gone, its replacement, a silk, vertically slotted shade was covering glass the length and breadth of the wall and already casting shadows of beautiful rhododendrons from my garden on the east side of the house.

If you are lucky, you too can stop to breathe in the view for a moment at any time in a busy day and the serendipitous, the unexpected, might just reach out and grab you by the heartstrings.

I turned off the skinny women pumping away unforeseen fat on TV exercise machines and the mattress demonstration with wine glasses full of what you might expect on such a hilarious occasion as grown men jumping up and down on a mattress like six-year-olds, knowing nothing is going to happen to upset those glasses full of wine glued before their eyes before the dinner bell rings.

I watch now, instead, every morning before rising, the miracles of Old Sol playing games in my garden and slowly making a fascinating shadow movie on my silken shade.

Waking up one morning at my usual time, 7:00 a.m., I look out my window to see that Old Sol is at work already and a couple of leaves on his painted shade are in the exact spot as they have been on previous mornings. So they tell me what time it is.

Through my whole life, thinking has been my hobby, and the best time to enjoy that pastime is lying in bed cozy and warm.

That same morning, head in the clouds, time passed away without notice until the same two silken leaves on the screen had moved down and away from their position at 7:00 a.m.

My thoughts moved back in time to an old stone structure called Stonehenge, a circle of pillars mysteriously erected around 250 BC, for what purpose it still is debated. Stonehenge!

This famous megalith has been a tourist attraction in southern England for many years, and when I walked around those huge stones, I experienced a chilly feeling, thinking of it like some people do today as a burial ground. But no one can claim proof of its purpose.

There is much guesswork going on, but no one has positive proof of a reason it was erected. The five possible reasons for the presence of Stonehenge in southern England are these:

A place of the dead
A place of healing
An astronomical observatory
Moon worship
A UFO landing place

My guess has always been on the scientific edge, a childish notion that its purpose was to monitor and register the rhythm and regularity of the sun's rays on those somber stones to prove that the time of its travel could be recorded in seconds, minutes, and hours, let alone years! Stepping stones in other words to marking time and mechanically recording the passing of it. (Some of my information is taken with thanks from Wikipedia.)

When all is said and done, I much prefer my window as a time-teller rather than a ring of stubborn stone-cold pillars.

And surely even the Secular Order of Druids, who were known for suspicious behavior within the area of Stonehenge, might have been involved in such a project. The pronunciation of this ancient order of nonbelievers was shortened to SOD by the English, and Father told me that bad people were called SODS and that it was a swear word and never to use it.

And this is the first time I ever did.

Of course new mysteries difficult to understand are still popping up in this electronic age of miracles.

For instance I was amazed last evening watching a TV show where a huge illuminated tent structure was reflecting images moving up and down and floating around in the air like balloons. I looked up in wonderment, realizing it was all a reflection of real live people dancing around outside of the magically enlightened tent, holding firm to terra firma.

I became young again, and wished I could sprout wings to fly up there and show them how to dance the foxtrot.

But later, as I looked in the mirror I was amazed to see all these deeply implanted furrows around my face.

"Now where did all of those come from overnight?"

I keep on looking and thinking. Then comes that knowing flash of light in the dark, the heart lifting emotion, hope … hope that the sight in my failing right eye is improving, and I am seeing something I haven't even noticed before now. I am just a little older than I was yesterday.

THE GHOST OF OLD TIM CONWAY

Mirror, Mirror on the Wall,
Who's the fairest of them all?

Reflecting on images brings up another short-term memory occasion regarding truth and beauty that I wish to get off my chest.

"If you grow old gracefully with good intensions, a kind heart, and a sense of humor, you might live to be one hundred," my father would tell me repeatedly. And here I am, almost a centenarian, whispering, "Mirror, mirror on the wall, who is the fairest of them all?"

A pensive mood shrouded my brain as I minced my way from the bed toward the mirrored closet doors, careful not to trip over my nightgown in the process.

"You should have been at your computer long before now, documenting these brilliant observations before they crawl away to sleep forever in that short-term memory bank of yours," I was thinking aloud.

A few more beleaguered breaths, the mind still preoccupied with sweet dreams, the mirror was before me. I reached up a hand to brush my fingers through the straggling hairs lagging over the eyes to see if I looked respectable enough to face a world ready for the challenges of another day.

But the image staring through the mirror before me could never belong to me! It was some shrunken old man in a nightshirt. Old bones, old wrinkles, eyes narrowed and squinting for a better view, tousled gray hair, a puzzled childish grimace on his face, his neck twisting right, then left, surveying the room for the safest route to the door like a cat in a roomful of rockers, knowing not what on earth he was supposedly doing, or where he was going, his back bent forward, as if old age was creeping up on him, as it had happened to me.

Oh my! What if that pitiful body was really mine reflected there? I didn't know whether to laugh or to cry. But in a flash, the picture became clear, then a chuckle started to rise and the laughter won out.

Tim Conway himself would agree that I was the spitting image of him acting the part of a confused old man in one of the never-to-be-forgotten Carol Burnett television comedies.

And there I was, a caricature of Tim Conway in a nightshirt! I went back to the mirror once more that day just for a chance to laugh out loud at myself rather than the brilliant comedian who has mimicked many personalities in his acting career but never came face to face with a face like mine.

How well I remember those old Carol Burnett shows. Humor can be the best medicine in the world, and I've been known to keep a bottle of it on the kitchen shelf for times like this when pride comes before a fall.

CHAPTER XVII

GROWING OLD GRACEFULLY

Someone once wrote, "Senescence begins and middle age ends the day your descendants outnumber your friends."

I don't believe everything I read, and no, this isn't the story of a senescent soul of ninety years still mourning beloved relatives buried on the other side of the Atlantic Ocean. I am the only living leaf on the Hope side of our family tree and admit to a lack of time and interest to sit in a rocking chair totting up all my friends in relation to my descendants, those who have hung there on its branches before me and my own offspring who will ascend after I am gone. No matter who enters my home, Mother, becomes my friend sooner or later.

I have taken many strolls down the garden path on the promise of a rose garden, and sadly have ended up in the compost heap, but I have discovered a certain kind of peace in my later years. Whatever has gone before shall stay behind, the dark side forgotten and thus forgiven.

The joys I find today come from breathing in that which we can see and feel and hear from this good earth, the living, the dying, and the rebirth of all things bright and beautiful.

I have amassed a crowd of friends who become more precious and abundant as the years slip by, but one can't sit at home twiddling the thumbs, expecting them at a beck and call. You have to get out and about to keep in touch with the world singlehandedly, and you will find that you can.

Life can become very lonely when widowhood strings one along into empty space. So if you are wise, you get out and about regardless of aches and pains. Or maybe you can invite the neighbors over, old or young.

THE VERY IMAGE

My youngest friend, Nick, who is now in high school, stopped by the other day and brought his very young pet llama, Poncho, to visit me, and we all huddled together on the front step, Nick smiling proudly, and as I thought, trying to hum a tune. But after a while, I was seriously advised that I wasn't hearing Nick singing through his nose. It was the darling baby llama trying to talk with me, because "that's what llamas do, Irene … they hum!"

It was a short visit, but it taught me how a young boy might love animals. He proudly told me how tall and proud Poncho would grow, adding, "See, he's almost as tall as you are, and I'm training him already." To which Poncho added a few short snorts.

A long-time 4H member, Nick had shown llamas at public ceremonies, walked with them in memorial parades, and put them through their paces to win ribbons in 4-H competitions.

As they turned away, Nick guiding Poncho with his arm around the neck, the llama came to a full stop, and Nick could not budge him. Every time Nick pulled on his rein, Poncho would stand his ground and turn his head to look through my bay window, as if he were mesmerized.

He was seeing his beautiful reflection in the glass, and I swear I saw him smile. On second glance, he may have thought the reflection was his mother waiting for him inside my house.

His latest showmanship with Zimbellie was to win Best of Show, a heart-warming occasion for me, and I was brave enough to stroke this endearing animal's soft and silky coat. It isn't a sin, Mother, to love all animals and to list them among your friends.

KEEPING APPOINTMENTS

A wise woman never yields to appointment.
—Stendhal
(good advice)

It took me more than a few seconds to recognize the humor in those few words—they are all between the lines!

Speaking of appointments, I would rather not, and often wish time would tick back to the era when you thought your sniffling child was in the throes of something life-threatening. You simply picked up the phone (if you could afford to own one) and tried to speak in controlled and intelligent manner, you said, "Hi, doc, would you mind stopping by and checking on my youngest?"

After a few medical inquiries on your infant's symptoms, he would reassuringly stifle your fears with, "It doesn't sound like anything serious, Irene. I'll stop by and take a look."

It was the simplicity of communication during those years that brought about the well-known phrase, "The customer is always right."

The voice of the people today is merely a whisper in a deaf ear, for instance in the business world where one is "put on hold" by companies large or small when trying to connect you with whomever can answer your plea for service. Often so long that I fall asleep to the sound of poor-choice music or a boring spiel about what the company can do for me if only I am a good girl and can wait at their convenience. And all in an unconvincing and out of tune voice.

At this moment, Mother, I am back at the fish stall on Buttermarket Street with you, hearing the shrill voice of the fisherwoman as she slaps a hunk of common cod in a piece of the *Manchester Guardian*, saying, "That's all the catch we got, luv," while Father is home waiting for his favorite halibut. I don't call that customer satisfaction one jot, especially when the halibut is lying in wait at the back of the stall.

And it happens all of the time here today, full staff too busy to accommodate you saying, "Please hold. Our lines are all busy at the moment. Your call will be answered in the order it was received. Please hold ... your business means a lot to us ... please hold ... please hold ... please enter the last four digits ... " until I'm ready to ring 911 or wring somebody's neck! Busy, busy phone lines and myself a busybody, old woman when I ask politely why I can't ask somebody a simple question.

And when I ask, in desperation, to speak to the manager— please hold—"he's with another customer at the moment," or "he is out to lunch," "not at his desk," or over in Timbuktu on a business trip! Monkey business?

Don't tell me they are feeling the economic crunch with so much business going on while I wait with ear-piercing music blaring at me.

And have you noticed the diminished size of bottled, bagged, and boxed products in the last year or so? Smaller containers with match-size content, yet prices still rise for profit and not for reimbursement for sacked employees, with millions of unemployed people begging back their jobs, which were sacrificed to greed and riches.

I could share much more in regard to how this situation is detrimental to old widows with very short-term memory, but one can't afford to hold grudges, and I tend to forget there are millions more than I who are tying to save for a rainy day. But take it from me, its been raining every day in Corvallis, Oregon, where I live, here in Paradise where infinity was born.

Beautiful flowers and a Japanese maple in the back yard. What price beauty? You don't have to pay for it here. Fruits and vegetables all ripe in their season, and some kind souls are producing them now to give freely for families in need.

You meet some people you hold as friends after one meeting, and you treasure the time spent with them.

Bennie is one of that kind.

Her father, expecting a boy, had his heart set on calling him Benjamin, or Benny for short, so Mother Fry placated him by calling their beautiful daughter Bennie, my new friend.

Here in beautiful Corvallis, Oregon, we live a few miles apart, but how do I love this age of hot, speedy communication. Mother, you would be awestruck to see your great-great grandson on my Apple computer, full screen. He will be two years old on Thanksgiving Day, a happy, intelligent young man who is a joy to watch grow and to learn from miles away in Rhode Island. I always wanted a brother.

CHAPTER XVIII

A WEEK OF WOES AND NO SHOWS

"Woe is wondrously clinging: the clouds roll by." This anonymous aphorism I take with a pinch of salt.

I knew it had to be Monday. The blues set in the minute I got out of bed and dressed, at least as far as the stocking maneuver, which I thought had been mastered to the nth degree.

While gloating over the fact that I now could accomplish the feat of shoving my feet into support hose while in the prone position, I decided to sit on the side of the bed, bend down, and slide on those party-pooper pressure partners one at a time.

Oh, I did it all right—at least I got one foot on—accompanied by the blaring screech of my Life Alert necklace, which had somehow become tangled up with my bra and was squeezed against my midriff hard enough to set off the alarm. I thought I was hearing an air raid siren.

Off to the kitchen I waltzed, all hunched over, waited at least one second for the Alert people in Albany say, "Irene Hedrick, do you need help?" Did I ever! But sheepishly I said, "Oh, no thank you. No accident, it was just my alert button sounding off accidentally when it shouldn't."

Never in a million years did I want a male dashing over to rescue me from the mischief a bra had caused. It was just the other day I learned what the English call a demi- bra ... one cup.

Well, now completely frustrated and a whole blue day in front of me, I put my cup in the microwave when I remembered I had unplugged the thing the day before since it was emitting hot air from a leak somewhere.

Come to think of it, Sunday too had been a blues Monday, because I got lost on the Internet again right in the middle of ordering a lovely new microwave. On sale, too—right size, right color, thirty dollars off, which actually was a guise to offset the thirty dollar mailing freebie from the day before, which today was my responsibility to pay, since I was getting a thirty-dollar rebate.

Tuesday wafted in on a good note and scrambled away with nothing accomplished except to remember it was Tuesday.

Wednesday I came across this neatly typed manuscript loosely tucked into a green construction paper cover stenciled with the words "My Autobiography" by Dan Hedrick.

Dan was then our youngest son, having celebrated his tenth birthday on June 6, 1965, when international conglomerations were allowed to enter the fair, for the first time competing in New York City to show their prowess and persuasions to the rest of the world.

My husband had taken us to see the sights in New York City and to visualize the possibility of incredible inventions of the future for us to dream on at the fair, which would now be named the World Fair. Not by plane, not by train, and an absolute *not* by bus, but we all squeezed up with the luggage in our tiny Volkswagen Beetle. He and I, Hope-Anne, and Dan went. Haydn, who was a senior in high school, was allowed to stay home and look after the dog and other necessities we didn't think of. Like throwing a party! He let us know when we arrived home that he had contacted a friendly neighbor we all knew and loved, a policeman to whom he had confided he was having some boys over for a get-together and to let them know if they were making too much noise. How's that for police protection?

But back to New York City. Hope had been designated to read the maps, and she did a great job, except, from no fault of her own, we ended up entering NY on the shady side, and we must have crossed the George Washington Bridge three times before heading up town, whichever way Ray decided that would be.

We cruised into Madison Avenue and turned off right to find a hotel for the night. Then the circus of ignorance broke loose as I heard a whistle blowing, and there was a policeman running fast as any harrier I knew. Ray finally stopped the car, and I lowered the window. "Where the h*** do you folks think you are going," he screamed in my ear. "You're going the wrong way on a one-way street!" He must have thought we were from Dogpatch when my husband leaned over and meekly made his apology. "Sorry, sir. We're just fresh in from Montana."

Can you imagine a surge of traffic being held up by an officer, while a Beetle turned its back on those snooty limousines and sporty English MGs and herded them onto the right of way?

Dan's autobiography was a longer piece than most students write today with the computer and the Internet handy. If I remember correctly in those past years, colored television was the rage of the age. What a wonder to behold. And I never even imagined then that I would be watching my great grandchild on my Mac computer screen, learning to walk and talk over the air from Rhode Island.

I would like to share some of Dan's thoughts, feelings, and experiences to give you a few pointers on what might have emerged from imagination to realization in the present day.

The first part is an account of his birthday and his childhood as a student, starting in kindergarten, where he wrote, "I had my first girlfriend when I was six. I thought that I had to start early to get ahead."

How well I remember that, Dan. You brought her home so she could teach you how to skip, and there you were, happily hopping around the kitchen table, hand in hand, and you asked if she could stay for lunch "since she was already there."

He writes about his pets: "My first pet was a cat named Blacky." And I thought Blacky was his dog all these years, the one who bit Hope's nose.

He mentions Chauncy, the family dog who gradually became his dog. "Chauncy's favorite sport was chasing birds and airplanes. He was a fast runner and could almost outrun a plane. One day I just set out some food when an airplane came over. He ran a couple of feet, paused, and couldn't decide which to go after. Finally he ran after the plane and came back to get his food later.

"In summer," he goes on, "I explore the hills in Makoshika Park, trying to find caves and neat places. My friends and I found such places like Fossil Land, the Shack, Rattlesnake Cave, Coal Cave, Three Caves." Then he says, "To comfort those who are afraid of snakes, and mothers who won't let kids go out there because of snakes, I have explored the hills for five years and have only seen one snake. As a matter of fact, I have seen more inside of the city limits."

I'd like to share a few more highlights from my son's autobiography, and you can see how the world has changed from those awe inspiring days. My youngest wrote, "I climbed to the top of the Empire State Building. We went through the Museum of Natural History and saw Rembrandt and Renoir's famous paintings. I stood on a moving platform to see the Pieta. I also saw mummy caskets and mummies. On a boat to the Statue of Liberty, we passed a car junkyard, and the driver said it was what was left of the Women's Driving School. At the World Fair, I saw the IBM building. It was shaped like a giant egg." I just don't remember that awe-inspiring place from inside.

He remembered seeing every kind of modern communications in the world there that day.

He wrote, "Next we went through Japan's Pavilion and saw some of Japan's famous things." Apparently he wasn't too interested and didn't remember why they were so famous, because that was his only sentence on that subject.

Speaking for myself, I remember seeing the beauty that Japan held, the grace and courtesies the people exhibited, and as the years have gone by, they have definitely made an impression on me with their works of wonder. And to think we are making all this to-do of certain countries making threats with nuclear weapons, and we are still the only country in the world that has ever used that destructive device in real time war?

Dan goes on to describe one architectural marvel. He says, "There was a large café under the top floor with a map of New York built right in the floor." I do remember that but not the name of the building.

Another of his descriptions of the World Fair: "We had shrimp at the cost of $12 for the four of us."

All I can definitely remember was that it took us an hour and forty-five minutes just to get inside the General Motors building. My son gives us much more information. He relates, "The exhibit was of the future. It had a machine that would go through tropical rain forests, making trees, bushes, and vines into pavement. In back of THIS machine, there was a machine that would make the pavement into a four-lane highway. The presentation also showed how it would look under the sea in compressed houses. Then it showed how it would look on the moon and how transportation was going to be. It showed us the history of every General Motors car. I liked this the best." I could see that. That's why today he's driving a top-of-the-line Honda, pure white, with gadgets you'd never believe.

He goes on, "Next we went into the science building. It had a real neat science room with neat gadgets. We didn't know it, but we were being watched by our parents while we were trying out the gadgets." Hmm, I would never have allowed them in there otherwise.

"We went into the space rocket, and it told about the human body ..."

And, darn, that's where this neat story ends for me. The rest of it was nowhere to be found.

CHAPTER XIX

MOVIES AND SUCH

"Apart from blunt truth, our lives sink decadently amid the perfumes of hints and suggestions."

Whitehead coined those wise words, Mother, and I believe the men and women who are responsible for our country's wellbeing today should think on them without prejudice.

Ever since the era of silent pictures, which brought on nightmares after reading horror show scripts for Granny Knight's pleasure, I have chosen my movies very carefully: *My Three Sons, Mrs. Miniver, Educating Rita, Julia, Gone with the Wind,* and *The King's Speech* for example

But sorry to say, on par with *Knocked Up*, the present generation of movie moguls has premiered such titles as *And Then She Found Me,* and, for goodness sake, again, *Knocked Up,* where anything goes either on or off, and like many films today, in one ear and out the other with no thumbs-up in appreciation.

Thumbs must be so overworked nowadays, as they have become permanently captivated by every new pod within their reach, except, of course, the pea pod.

Yet I am very proud to own a beautiful Mac computer on which to write my thoughts and happy as a lark to be still living and enjoying the fruits of this electronic age.

Never in my dreams have I ever had such a thrill and have never given a thought that I might witness even a few of the futuristic possibilities that were premiered at the World Fair so long ago.

In the first place, I didn't imagine I would be typing onto a screen, using an ultra-modern keyboard without an eraser at hand. As a matter of fact, I've actually been known to unscrew the Wite-Out bottle top and nearly daub a brush full of Wite-Out over a typo in this do-it-yourself document.

I thought I was getting used to all of these magical means of communicating, but lo and behold ...

My grandson had driven down from Portland last Sunday to help me sort out which button goes where and does what with my new computer, a large-screen Mac, which in English means a raincoat.

We spent a pleasant day together, me watching the Blazers, and he enjoying what he loves most—tinkering with computers. We had dinner out as soon as Dan had developed a few tutorials to guide me. Everything was fixed, even learning how to so easily make the cards I used to make on my old PC with Home Publishing.

I learned one important thing about this all-in-one piece of equipment: as soon as you learn what to push and click, or kick, a Mac does the work for you.

However, left alone again I panicked, squinting at what the tiny icons across the top of the screen read and wondering how to whip back into line the huge icons jumping up and down on my Scrabble game, which I thought would calm me down.

The hopeless feeling I was going through took me back to that never-to-be-forgotten error of sending one hundred copies of my written word to someone I really respected.

So I thought I would try to use Jabber. I've done that before with my grandson but never tried the other option on that particular means of communicating with him.

As luck would have it, I accidently clicked one of the other options beside texting and quickly heard a male voice I recognized as Dan's. More than that, there was my grandson's face appearing on screen, laughing at me when I squeaked out, "Can you see *me.*" He held up a glass, taking a sip, "Here's to you, Gran. I see you're having a sip at a nightcap, too."

Now, what's your problem, grandmother?

It was evident to Dan that I had short-term memory problems as I tried to think of how to describe the actual ones, so he said, "I'll get on your desktop and see what I can do." I watched the cursor scurrying over the screen at random with no guidance by anyone I could see, making corrections wherever they may have been.

Then I heard, "Night, night, Gran. And get to bed early. Next time I come to visit, we can have a fireside chat with your new great grandson in Rhode Island, and see what he is up to."

Before I turned in, I did what I do every night. I turned on Flickr to see activated camera shots my son-in-law makes of Isaac, my first great grandson, and I go through this one time and time again.

He is sitting on the floor, thumbing through a small book. He scrambles up and starts running, making the noise of a fire engine and holding the book high in his hand screeching, "Mommmmm, Mommmmm" and a few more words that couldn't come out right. But the action itself tells the story.

His father's voice can be heard saying, "Mom's taking a bath, Ikey." Isaac stops, book still waving before a closed door in the hallway, raising the other hand, he tries to reach the doorknob. That didn't work.

After ruffling through the book's pages again, still shouting, "Moooom, Mooom," he tries to push in the door. Still no movement from the door. So he knocks, politely, and the door slowly opens, and you know mom is right there to see the fire engine in his book. He turns to look at his dad, and I see both tears and laughter in his beautiful brown eyes.

What a wonderful world it is, and how happy I am to be alive in this electronic age that was once a mere thought.

ALL ABOUT JAM

Actually, not jam of the fruity variety, but "Just Another Movie" jamboree, a spicy, some would say luscious, raspberry jam movie for those who might swallow it whole, relishing the sight, sound, and sensual impact of it to the point of licking their fingers of the remnants, all without choking on the seeds of malfeasance buried inside each luscious berry.

I really don't know where to begin; it's bothered me for so many years! But I just have to get it all out of my system, which can't take knocks of any kind any more. The movie was called *Knocked Up*.

When I think about the subliminal message of the media with its nauseating undertones of sex beckoning a come-on to gullible customers, it pushes the button of my tolerance, especially when scanning the television screen for a decent movie that might put me to sleep.

I suppose it all goes back to my upbringing and my mother, Emily Knight Hope, the exemplification of biblical truth, which she practically shoved down the throats of her four daughters. In fact she sent us to church school to learn firsthand the sacred writings in the Bible she cherished, and when the vicar asked our class one day who wrote the *Book of Proverbs*, my hand shot up, and I shouted out before I was even called upon, "My mother did."

Looking back on it though, she never would explain the word "covet" in the ten commandments to me, and she brushed it aside saying, "I've already told you that the grass is greener on the other side of the hedge, haven't I? That's exactly what covet means." She never dreamed of telling any one of us the facts of life face-to-face, just vague warnings about staying away from boys! But somehow, somewhere, from somebody, we four girls figured out that boys and girls together made babies. Well, we all four loved babies. We had to sit them so much, but then I loved wildflowers even more and didn't have time for boys.

But I'd better backtrack to my caustic discussion of a movie that churned my stomach to sour cream. After a first-class dinner at Le Bistro last Saturday, during my daughter's visit, we ended up at Carmike Cinemas, having decided to see the only movie the *Gazette Entertainer* touted worthy of watching.

I beg to differ from the newspaper's favorable review

Knocked Up! I thought that *must* be some kind of comedy with a joke, with that as the title and the leading lady a blonde, innocent-looking beauty who had done herself wrong but turned out all right in the end.

And so, comfortably seated on the front row of the upper section, I relaxed, ready to fall asleep if need be, but no need to worry about that!

LIGHTS! CAMERA! ACTION!

Though action was hardly the word to use! A group of young men wasting away their lives smoking pot, drinking I know not what, foul-mouthed, disgusting f-word language every other word, slurring from uncultured minds through sluggish tongues, making no sense whatsoever. You might say a group not at all as impressive as they tried to portray. What a disappointment, not a hero amongst them.

Then into the picture come two innocent-looking blondes: one strikingly beautiful to behold, the other a little coarser looking, a trifle older and wiser, but both on the same level of perceived intelligence. Wow!

Talk about the fallen angel. I didn't even care if our heroine was wearing wings or if she had a first or a second name, she was absolutely wantonly wanting and not wanting to wait, and the whole scenario of sex and the complexity of condoms blatantly pictured for our benefit, with heroine and fly-by-night hero in full-screen view, cavorting before an expected audience of stand-ins experienced with the sexual arts, who might have gladly joined them in spite of the foregone conclusions, to wit, "Oh, dear God, help me. I think I am pregnant and have to get rid of this unexpected little being whose father is a big time loser."

At that point I wanted to vomit and to lock her behind closet doors. I didn't care to wait and see what else befell this supposedly innocent creature conceived by some playwright's playfully twisted mind. He probably gave no thought that an eighty-seven-year-old woman might be inquisitive enough to see what kind of a knockout the *Knocked Up* movie might be.

What a waste of human energy by two people seeking instant gratification and accomplishing nothing more productive and worthwhile in this life than oohs and aahs and a few dying echoes from the Garden of Eden. Just think of all that productive energy wasted away that could have been put to better purpose in life. Art, music, architecture, writing, earning a living rather than so-called loving. My daughter and I had exchanged sidelong glances in the dimmed theater, jerking our heads in the direction of the exit a couple of times, hesitantly suffering through Act II of the bare-bottomed heroine's toilet-sitting attempts while gulping down quarts of pungent potions to rid herself of the load she wasn't about to carry, in order to re-establish our poor heroine's claim of unadulterated innocence.

Then came the extravaganza of the latex-glove probing to verify a pregnancy, and I could stomach no more. My daughter and I bravely headed for the exit with not a backward nor an upward glance and went home to watch the last ten minutes of my favorite Pistons "losing their bid for another national basketball championship" to a lesser team whose star character was worth his salt and lived up to everybody's expectations.

I've thought a lot about that movie, wondering about present-day relationships and the preponderance of unwed, unwise, and once-upon-a-time unlawful cohabitations resulting from such easy-come, easy-go behavior. I remember in the olden days, we called them common-law marriages if they extended beyond a one-night stand, and the cause and effects of the practice were rarely brought to light, because they were considered to be morally insensitive and people shunned the perpetrators. Sexual activity nowadays seems to be heading in the direction of Aldus Huxley's futuristic look at the waywardness of it in his once-popular books portraying sexuality as merely sex and nothing more.

What if the silken sheets of love and honor become split during these live-in acquaintances when the flames of desire start to flicker, and the grass really becomes greener over that high board fence? A quick, easy separation without any legal proof of responsibility might possibly leave one or the other party in the lurch holding an empty purse, the bag of bugaboos, and the baby. What a coming-out party for a little one to start out on the right foot. What price freedom? God Bless America. She gives me the freedom to try that myself, if ever I have a mind to!

Divorce was considered a scandalous affair in the olden days, but could I have had a happier life in a partnership without benefit of clergy?

Common sense tells me no, I might have kept on making the same mistakes.

Because I believe we fashion our selfhood, our personal mythology, by the choices we make throughout our lives, and often they are made haphazardly, with little thought of consequence, like I did.

There came a day in my life when I asked my eldest son hat the right choice was to make in a risky situation. He gave me one of those looks that sons reserve especially for their parents and said, "Mother! No one has ever made a right choice. First, you make a choice. And then you make it right. Right? I've lived on that premise for all the ever after, so far. First, I make a choice, and *then* I do my best to make it right." Best advice I ever received in spite of what's happened in my own life.

I try to pass this on to my intellectual thirteen-year-old grandson Spencer, along with the teachings of psychologist Viktor

Frankl's philosophy with which he gave hope to those facing death in the gas chambers during World War II.

He told them that even though he had been stripped of all material things, he ever owned *one thing* they could *never* take from him. And that thing, he said, is the attitude one decides to take in any given situation.

I've benefited from that advice, too, helping me on to one hundred years old.

A DARK AND SINISTER STORY

Do any of you youngsters remember Ronald McDonald? The TV clown? I knew him personally, but not through the McDonald's care facility, and his good work brought smiles to sick children's faces.

He was equally famous as a member of the National Speakers Association, first and foremost, and did the charity spiel in the hamburger joint venture just for the heck of it, because he loved people.

He was a brilliant speaker, and I had the chance to become acquainted with him as a fellow member of National Speakers Association when I was attending a Montana School Board Association long ago.

It was there that I learned from him about a small boy with lots of spunk but with no means to let it rise and shine, and no one to tell him that he had rickets. That's an old-time disease, once thought incurable, but this young boy was taken to heart by a doctor who loved the boy's determination to play sports, even though the gentleman would tell him over and again, "You will never play sports, son. You have rickets disease." But the lad would stand up straight and, with all his might, pull back his shoulders and proudly, deliberately say, "Oh, yes, I will! I *love* football!"

Yes, it *was*, O. J. Simpson, our hero, the running back Heisman Trophy winner playing on Oregon State University's football team and, even more commendable, winner of young hearts, thousands of them who wished to follow in his footprints to the end zone of success, their hopes trampled underfoot with the autumn leaves of football seasons.

What went wrong, O. J.?

Was it the money? Was it the fame? Was it the thrill of the wind at your back, pushing you ever forward to your never-ending goals? Or did you plain and simply stop pursuing your bliss and drop the precious ball you have carried so far. How in this world could you go wrong, if you really have done wrong O. J? I'm puzzled now, because you sound like all the good stuff has been kicked out of you as you followed your dream to the end zone.

If you are guilty, you have, by your actions, proved that a lawyer can become a millionaire just by playing a game on your team.

If you are indeed innocent, are you now playing some other more sinister game in defiance of the law?

Anyway, O. J., if you possibly have thought to regain the wealth you lost by writing a book, you have my sympathy.

CASH AND CARRY

Though a good deed is strange to believe, nothing is too strange to have happened.
—Thomas Hardy

Old women often are handicapped with what are called short-term memories, and I am such a one. So naturally, I must begin with the most recent tales from my life without pause from their happening, in case my long-term memory dies before I do.

Between you and me, I am old enough to have a great grandson born on Thanksgiving Day while my oldest son was visiting, making two reasons to give thanks for the good things in life besides the turkey on that particular day in 2001.

Haydn is usually very careful with his spare change and how he spends it, but the morning before the holiday, he had carelessly stuffed a roll of hundred dollar bills in a rubber band into his jacket pocket before taking a tour of the beautiful city of Corvallis in Oregon.

He was removing his jacket, and I saw a frown on his face. He was hollering at me, "Mother, my money—it's gone!"

I helped him search the house, with no results, so we went through his whereabouts during the course of the day to our last stop at Fred Meyers.

I had the unhappy thought that might be the most probable place for a roll of dough to slip out of a jacket pocket, since the aisles at the store were jammed with carts and people pushing them any which way in a last-minute rush to buy a turkey.

His thoughts had been going in that direction, and he was already on the phone, asking if any money had been found and turned in. The staff there assured him they would call back if they had any information for him.

Five minutes later, that they did, announcing the money had been found by an honest woman who turned it in.

They had obtained her phone number, since she was not a local customer, and passed it along to my son. He called to thank her, offering a handsome reward for her honesty in returning the money where she found it, but she politely refused to accept his generosity.

Haydn's story was the high point of Thanksgiving dinner as he raised a toast to the honest staff at our family-friendly Fred Meyers store where you can find everything you need, including lost cash returned by an honest customer who turned out to be a professor of law at Penn State University.

A FLASHBACK

Memories of a Big Sky British War Bride is receiving good reviews, I'm happy to say, but the one I truly treasure is passed on by my daughter from a friend of hers, a ninety-plus-year-old lady and still an avid reader. It was so delightful; I have to share it.

Hope was helping edit the page proofs for me and knew her friend would appreciate an opportunity to read the original thing. But after a few days, the lady called and said, "Hope, I loved your mother's memoir. It reads like a novel, but I just didn't understand the ending."

I spoke up, in defense, "Hope, that's strange. You haven't noticed anything misleading or out of context with all the other parts in your proofing have you?"

My daughter hesitated for a second and confessed, "Well, it's like this, Mom—I only gave her four chapters!"

The lady must have been frustrated, because the end of the fourth chapter in that book had left me nursing our newborn baby, and my husband was still out there in the waters of Flathead Lake determined to bring home a trout or two. The lady must have thought he was still on the lake rowing to his heart's content.

CHAPTER XX

A WORLD OF FOOD

"The discovery of a new dish does more for human happiness than the discovery of a new star," says a devoted French chef.

I tend to agree, but a new dish will more easily fall flat on its face while the star still shines in the heavens or lives on stage.

Bon appétit! I was hoping to meet Julia Child when my eighteen-year-old grandson Colin and I visited Paris on a Christmas holiday. No such luck, but I did fall in love with the food over there and relied on my companion's knowledge of French when necessary, except when he decided he fancied hamburgers or pizza, and I wanted fancier French meals. The second time he longed for home-baked American food, it really upset my applecart, and I told him he could dine alone. "But you don't know any French, Grandmother!" The way he would say grand-mother in such a dignified manner would usually get him anything he wanted, but this time I became a little huffy and said, "Oh, I'll do very well, thank you!" And I did.

I learned French from Julia Child. In fact I had always thought of her as being French, and I loved her personage, so it was a natural for me to speak French when it came to fine food. I told Colin I would first raise a toast to Julia with a fine glass of Bourgelais, then I would tackle the *boeuf* with a brut, a mousse for the *gateau*, and *fromage*, and what else could finish off a fine meal served by waiters who seemingly adored me but the crème de la crème of desserts, the burnt sugar thing, crème brûlée, along with a snifter of Grand Marnier and a cup of café au lait! My French improved steadily with practice, since Col went out for pizza quite a lot during those days along the Mediterranean. And he always brought home a mini pizza, in case I was too scared to go out alone!

The excitement of spending a romantic afternoon the next day with Renoir, Monet, and Manet at the Musée d'Orsay was more than enough for any creative spirit. The beauty of the impressionists' work was awe-inspiring, but there was more to come, for I had reserved dinner and theatre tickets at the *Moulin Rouge* since Colin had seen the movie and was curious to see it live. I said, "The real thing is for adults only, but what do I know when I have never witnessed what they show onstage. Let's go."

I became a little uneasy when we arrived at this show house of repute, because the crowd of want-to-sees spilling out into the street were pushing and pulling to get in and claim a seat.

The balcony dinner, served in true French style with a bucket of ice and a bottle of Champagne, lived up to its claim of excellence, but the show was nothing to drool about. The only noteworthy thing about it was to boast of going to Paris, and it was there.

Compared to the breathtaking beauty revealed by Manet's bold, yet so delicate, portrayal of a *Blonde with Bare Breasts*, the whole monty of the can-can sideshow at *Moulin Rouge*, with its brassy performers and brazen nudity, was no more appealing to me than a couple of poached eggs with a cherry on top.

Touring Versailles, in all its splendor, took up another whole day in our week's itinerary. It was a grand tour, if you took it all lightly, but I kept wondering why on earth a king would pamper his woman, Marie, by building her real dollhouses to keep her amused, yet when he speaks of his subjects going hungry for bread, she glibly tells him, "Then let them eat cake!" No wonder the French were forced to sell the royal furniture—made of pure silver—to pay for their everlasting wars.

We feel free when we escape—even if it be but from the frying pan into the fire.
—Hoffer

I didn't realize I had been getting old, until it dawned on me the need to be decisive about cleaning out and throwing away most of my books and newspaper clippings on a subject looked upon with great reverence and respect. They had accumulated, nestled together and hanging in there, on my library shelves for over seventy years.

You see, when I was young and fancy-free, it never did occur to me that loving food would be my destiny. For every bite that I consumed racked up another pound on me, whilst sneaking back for just one more delicacy.

You might say I lived to eat. Nor could I cease drinking in the TV master of cookery: Julia Child. In my first viewing, I watched closely to see her brandishing a hatchet held high with temerity and aplomb before bringing it down in one fell swoop with bone-crushing intent to meet the meat, as it were, of the poor carcass lying in wait on the cutting block.

I used to think she was French, until I read that she was a citizen of the USA, who had earned merit as a five-star French chef by working in their kitchens and communicating with them on the ins and outs of their trade.

I remember her sharp wit and good humor, especially in her later years when she would introduce other celebrity chefs to participate in her shows.

I shall never forget the Galloping Gourmet standing by her side, trying to help. Stirring up her hot, hot chili, Julia was challenging him to try it out.

He wasn't actually galloping at that moment but furtively approaching the cooking pot with good intent to please his hostess. Warily he lifted out a scant spoonful, barely opening his lips enough to let the beans slip through. Whereupon at the first taste of that devilish dish, and with hand up to mouth, he managed to choke out, "I've ... been ... violated!"

"Oh," Julia shot back coquettishly with pouting lip and blinking eyes, "I didn't know it was that easy!"

Nothing, not even losing long-term memory, could persuade me from throwing out her words of wisdom in the kitchen.

Like Pavarotti, the whole world mourns her absence, missing the aura of perfect performance that both had possessed and shared wholeheartedly to enrich our lives.

As for me, I would give up a whole day of my dwindling years for Pavarotti to sing just for me "La Donna E Mobile" live, one time more!

Jan Roberts Dominguez lives, cooks, writes, and paints in Corvallis, Oregon, where I also live, write, and paint but only wish I could cook as she does—expertly, especially with dishes dreamed up using Oregon's wonderful bounty of fruit, veggies, and nuts, along with seafood fresh from the Pacific Ocean a few miles west.

This young lady's expertise in the culinary arts is further enriched by her descriptive writings, which impart knowledge of food history, its preparation, its presentation, and its preservation—her beautiful artistry in watercolors also adding much more than a little relish and spice to all her endeavors.

I'll raise a toast to her with a glass of heartrending red wine this evening, and her recipes shall stay with me for sure.

Oh, to live to be a hundred! Here, in this paradise of Corvallis, Oregon.

Vincent Price first came into my kitchen as a well-known star-villain who eventually gave up the movies to become a food and wine connoisseur, traveling the world whilst collecting recipes and putting together a pictorial masterpiece medley of each nation's food-lovers' favorites.

His book has been special to me since the days when my friend and I entered legitimate contests sponsored by honest company executives who proved the excellence of their products by awarding worthwhile prizes to contestants for praising them. We won many prizes between us, including a first national award of a Ford station wagon for Carol and a third national prize in a Betty Crocker contest, coming my way in the form of a beautiful washer and dryer.

I can't remember the company who offered the Ford vehicle (and the toy model Ford for her child that went along with it), but it was a thrill for each of us to receive top prizes over a million and a half entries. My own challenge was sponsored by Betty Crocker, maker of the cakes that come in a box, asking the public to name her new kitchen. I don't suppose my entry will be blazed across her new kitchen doors, but I gave them the new name The Knack in the Box Kitchen.

Chapter XXI

ONCE UPON A COOKBOOK

I consider this precious cookbook an heirloom that will be passed along to my family.

My husband thought it would be a good start to figure out the art of cooking from those recipes he used.

I had survived the winter, summer, and fall of the year 1945 after my arrival in America, awaiting the return of my husband from his tour of duty in England.

He arrived ten days after our first child was born in Polson, Montana, deep in the heart of the Mission Mountains, where we eventually found a cabin on the Flathead Lake's West Shore to start a new life together with very short supplies and a one-and-only cookbook, which my husband said I must use until we could afford a new one.

My heart sank, because this precious book he had used as head chef of his company's mess hall at Burtonwood Royal Air Force base in Warrington, England, was designed to serve troops numbering three thousand or more clamoring through the mess hall doors and not a handful of two. The third member of our family, born October 11, 1945, was not on a solid food diet.

Back then, however, on a beautiful Indian summer day, the man in my family had announced he was going to borrow the landlord's rowboat to bring in a fish or two for dinner.

He stayed out there a long time, and I enjoyed my solitude, but eventually he was back. Tying up the rented boat to a tree at the water's edge, he ran into the house and threw a huge fish into the sink. "Here," he shouted, "clean 'er up. I'm going back out there!"

That fish stared me in the eye and dared me to touch it, so I gave it a little grace time to die properly before deciding what I should do with it. My first fish fry!

I picked up the much-fingered book titled the T.M. 10-412 War Department Technical Manual, *Army Recipes,* The War Department, 15 August 1944, used by him to satisfy the appetites of those in his care during his time at 509th Safety Squadron.

The first problem I had was to identify the kind of fish that lay there with its mouth sagging open as though begging for pardon. I flipped through the pages detailing awesome amounts of ingredients, finding recipes for salmon, haddock, halibut, and mackerel. Not a one for trout, which I guessed it to be, so I settled for Creamed Codfish, which sounded like a dish you might have concocted, Mother.

In the column of ingredients, I saw on that page that I needed to find "Codfish, salted, sixteen pounds" and "Toast, one hundred slices." This discouraged me from even trying to whittle down one hundred into two portions of everything, and, besides, how on earth does one skin a fish?

I left that trout where it lay and went to feed the baby, hoping my husband would come home in a mellow mood with a few more fish and feel obliged to do his own.

I have made several of the recipes from that sixty-nine-year-old cookbook, especially scalloped potatoes to honor a few good men who went AWOL and whose punishment for absence without leave was to sit outside the mess hall peeling hundreds of that vegetable to be scalloped and fed to the thousands of servicemen stationed at Burtonwood Royal Air Base.

THE WHITE HOUSE COOKBOOK

Hugo Ziemann
and
Mrs. F. L. Gillette

This White House Cookbook was compiled many years ago and is still in very good condition. It was handed down to me by a member of my husband's family, and I, too, wish to pass it along. It's even older than I am. It was published in 1907. I was born in 1920.

It is a wonderful book to browse over a cup of tea, and I love to sit by the fire reading it, loving the way the book's authors, Hugo Ziemann and Mrs. F. L. Gillette, describe the way things were prepared in the White House kitchen in 1907. The recipes aren't organized in systemized fashion as today but are in prose, like old wives' tales, as though they were sharing precious secrets from the bottom of their hearts. Just like your Stork Margarine cookbook that you treasured, Mother, since it was your only cookbook.

This American volume of cookery holds seven hundred pages with twenty-four index pages naming fascinating recipes, even medicinal cures, one of which was meant for people who needed to be fattened up called "Thinness."

"It is caused generally by lack of power in the digestive organs to digest and assimilate the fat-producing elements of food.

"First, to restore digestion, take plenty of sleep, take all the water the stomach will bear in the morning on rising, take moderate exercise in the open air, eat oatmeal, cracked wheat, graham mush, baked sweet apples, roasted and broiled beef, cultivate jolly people, and bathe daily."

It goes so far as to enumerate household hints and toiletry recipes you wouldn't believe, some of them made from an alcohol base. In fact if I do much more reading of this wonderfully inclusive book today, I won't have time to keep up my scheduled writing time. I might contact our president's gracious wife to have it reprinted and out on the bookshelves for everyone to enjoy.

WILL THE REAL BETTY CROCKER PLEASE STAND UP!

A retentive memory may be a good thing, but the ability to forget is the true token of greatness.
—*Elbert Hubert*

Retentive memory or not, I shall never forget *Betty Crocker's Picture Cook Book* because it has been within reach in my kitchen since day one.

You may have noticed that she has matured with the passing of time, because changes in her appearance have been made intentionally to keep up the aura of a warm, caring family mom cooking home-style, nutritious meals for the family named Crocker! It contains great illustrations to take you through the paces to produce perfect dishes from your kitchen.

Like me, you might have suspected the name Betty Crocker is a nom de plume for nobody in particular. Well, information from the Internet will confirm your belief that there is no such person. Actually, her image was designed from a collage of faces blended together from the living faces of women staff members, with the first image of Betty being changed periodically through the years since 1950 by adding the seasonings of old age to her face, still keeping the aura of Betty warm and friendly.

The first name was adopted from a female employee who had won a company contest. The last name, Crocker, was to honor retired General Mills executive William Crocker.

Next to Eleanor Roosevelt, Betty Crocker was the best-known woman in the interwar years.

Now that you know all about her, you can recommend her in good faith.

A FREE-FOR-ALL BETTY CROCKER LEMON MERINGUE PIE

"Even were a cook to cook a fly, he would keep the breast for himself."

This English proverb might have been penned by you, dear Mother, since you were so proud of all those concoctions you dreamed up. But you would never, ever allow a fly to hover over your frying pan, now would you?

Note: There is nothing proverbial about Betty's recipe for a truly luscious Lemon Meringue Pie. It is listed on page 363 of Betty's book and was always my youngest son's favorite dessert. I've made so many of them through the years I didn't need a recipe to guide me.

However, pride goeth before a fall. Now that I am old, Sara Lee and Mrs. Smith's sound much more enticing than spinning around the kitchen in circles with my vertigo, peripheral neuropathy, vestibular imbalance, acrophobia, high blood pressure, a blind eye, hearing impairment, and ingrown toenails to name a few of my infirmities.

Nowadays it takes me most of the day, hopping from one spot in the kitchen to another like a blue-bottle fly dodging a swatter, trying to find lost objects. I have just reorganized so that I could find them more easily, so there's not much time to start anything else, really.

But what does one do when the youngest son's birthday approaches and a couple of lemons are smiling at you from the counter. Oh well, an old-timer can do anything she likes in her own kitchen, and who cares? I used to bake his favorite lemon pie for every special occasion.

Well, here goes!

First, I need a magnifying glass so my eyes can read the recipe, and since it is not a kitchen utensil, I have to hunt for it in other places. The memory gets shorter with every passing day, and when you're pushing ninety, life is not always a bunch of cherries, especially when it comes to squeezing lemons larger than oranges, handpicked by loving friends on a trip to California.

I've been advised many times, "When life hands you a sour lemon, Irene, don't fret and upset your applecart! Make lemonade!"

Well, like most people, I have always loved lemonade, but wasting that precious fruit in a lemon drink recipe, when store-bought Kool-Aid would require no more effort than opening a package and turning on the faucet, was not my cup of tea.

So I decided yesterday that I might make one of those luscious lemon pies I used to make, which earned an honorable mention from my son Dan. And it would be nice to make a second pie as a thank you to Debby and John for the lemons.

I was what they called a housewife in those long-ago days, cooking for a family, guided by good basic recipes and pictures of how to master the art of cooking food fit for kings. Until this morning.

Talk about sour lemons! The hard, thick peel surrounding the good part was a tough nut to crack with arthritic fingers, so it became necessary to hunt down my wonderful drill-like, ridged lemon squeezer designed with a pointed end, rounding out like a toy top to a size large enough to twirl around inside half a lemon and squeeze out all that wonderful juice in a jiffy with a mere twist or two of the wrist. I begrudgingly took time out to find it and in the process forgot what I was looking for in the first place.

Splitting the eggs to separate yolk from white was not a problem the last time I tried. I merely tapped the egg sharply on the edge of a bowl and gently opened the split halves to let the white slip down and away from the yolk and into a bowl ready for whipping up a meringue.

The separated yolks then went into a separate bowl, one at a time, until all six eggs were accounted for.

What on earth has happened here today, I thought, as the yolks refused to stay resting where they belonged. The sharp edges of the broken shell were cutting into them so that they joined the whites in a mess that would be good only for a breakfast scramble. I gave up at egg number three and reluctantly dug out three more fresh eggs from the refrigerator to start all over again.

And then my memory kicked in, and I remembered Corinne's advice on the way she accomplishes that frustrating task.

"Oh, there's an easier way!" her voice is telling me. "I merely split the shell and let the whole egg plop gently into the bowl. After scrubbing my hands and drying them thoroughly, I cup one hand under the egg and scoop it up gently, letting the white stuff slip nonchalantly through my fingers and back down into the bowl."

It worked! And I had sense enough to tackle all six eggs two at a time.

I set about measuring sugar, lemon peel, cornstarch, butter, and water, beating the separated egg yolks and setting aside the whites ready for the meringue.

"OK. Now what?" It takes a few seconds for the tired old brain to keep up the routine, but oops! I forgot to take my morning pills, all twelve, two at a time, so I painfully get them down the throat and spot the scribbled note beside the pill bottles to remind me to "make the pastry next."

Believe me, things like that happen to octogenarians all of the time, but if you are like me, you don't really mind, because all you want to do in your life now is to make people happy.

In the past year or so, my pastry hasn't brought any raves from family or friends—I blame it on the ingredients—so I turned to Betty Crocker this time, believing that her guidance was just what a wandering eighty-nine-year-old mind needed to master the job at hand.

All went well, sifting flour and salt, blending in the butter just as her hands demonstrated in the pictures, but when the amount of water was added, there was no adherence of the ingredients whatsoever.

It was only then that I realized I had been measuring what I had always done before, doubling the recipe to fill two nine-inch pie plates. Except, when it came time to add the butter, I had already forgotten I was making two pies and calculated in the mere two-thirds cup of butter needed in the book's one-pie recipe.

My dreams of ever becoming a gourmet cook in my remaining years went down the drain with the eggshells, as I wondered how two-thirds cup of extra butter could ever be distributed evenly through the mixed mess waiting in the bowl.

The extra butter finally settled in the ball of dough in much larger chunks than warranted, but it finally attained the semblance of good pie dough and rolled out easily enough to fill two pie plates. So I crossed my fingers and set both pies in the oven at four hundred degrees to do as they pleased with my strenuous morning's work.

After putting all of my attention to cooking the filling, and completing that chore easily enough, I thanked God that the morning had finally ended satisfactorily. But wait! For the pastry had shrunk in the cooking and didn't look light and flaky as pastry should. As it cooled, I tried to break off a tiny piece for a taste test, and I'm ashamed to confess that it wouldn't even break away. Hard as nails it was, and when the whole crust slid out of the pie pan onto the kitchen floor with a thud, not a crumb was disturbed. I suppose you can guess I was devastated.

That evening a couple of friends took me to see a movie, so I invited them after the show to come and share the lemon pudding with the perfect peaks of lightly browned meringue on top.

The table was set and the teakettle was whistling, but the dessert was a total flop. The meringue had sadly sunk down into the pudding while waiting in the refrigerator, and the whole thing looked like a bright yellow sunlit ocean with whiffs of white foam floating the waves.

I was ready to cry or to blush with shame as my company glanced at one another and tried to keep a straight face.

I managed to keep the stiff upper lip of a true Brit and make the most of the situation by demonstrating how lightly I could handle it. So, picking up the empty pie shell from its pan on the counter, I handed it to Ron.

"Here, Ron, give it a few bangs on the fridge and see what happens."

The harder the pastry met the refrigerator door, the louder we laughed, until I was wiping my eyes with my apron. The crust still held the shape of the pan from which it came.

My friends came to the rescue, as they always do, agreeing to try out the pudding, regardless of its appearance. We argued on its demerits in very good humor, boosting my belief in the truth of that biblical phrase, "A merry heart doeth good, like medicine." I could have put off the pills for that day!

To heck with lemonade. I'll ask for peaches next time Debby and John visit California.

The movie we had seen, *And Then She Found Me*, had been a sour lemon, too. So I entertained my young guests with a few more old wives' tales, so they could avoid similar disasters when they reach the ripe old age of an octogenarian. This is the kind of freedom, the joys of living long, that gives me the courage to be myself and know myself. As I am and not whom I wish to be.

With a mischievous smile in his eyes, friend Ron's last words for the evening were: "What on earth would we men do without women?"

I just couldn't resist giving him the correct answer. "Nothing! You wouldn't be here!" I give Mark Twain honors for that witty remark. But how true it was and always shall be.

FISH AND CHIPS

Another cookbook I treasure is the first and only one you ever used, Mother, along with the dishes you dreamed up with the scanty ingredients allowed us with food stamp books during the Second World War. I still own and treasure that book.

If you remember, it has a picture of a stork on its old worn cover, and when I was growing up, I wondered what a stork would be doing on a cookbook when he was supposed to be delivering babies. It was called *The Art of Home Cooking* published by the Stork Margarine Cookery Service.

All I knew about cookery early in my life was that potatoes made chips, and bread and condensed milk miraculously produced a dish called *pobs*.

Mother's stoic disposition during the strike-ridden years of the 1920s, when Father's paychecks ceased to be, taught her four daughters to believe that fish and chips, a jam *buttie*, and a cup of tea made a meal fit for a king.

A few years ago, when our Ike, my sister Joyce, was hospitalized in England, I would call her from America, and we would chat about old times.

On the night before she died, her last words were, "Remember when we were kids when our I and poor our Em used to mix packet suet with water until it was stodgy, pat it all together, roll it in a tea towel, fasten it up with a safety pin, boil it for a couple of hours, and then slice it up and serve it to us with Tate and Lyle's Golden Syrup over it? We loved it."

When Joyce became tired of talking, she said, "I don't feel very well, luv. I'm going to sleep now, our I." And I find myself saying "'Twill be all right come mornin', luv." She died peacefully during the night.

THE TOOTH THE FAIRY DID NOT FIND

Our actions are neither so good nor so evil as our impulses.
—Vauvenargues

How true, I think, hoping my conclusions end up in harmony with the author of that aphorism.

It's a jolly good thing my hands were clean on that memorable day way back, when my daughter Hope was sitting in her highchair in the kitchen, banging a spoon on the wooden tray, and wanting to get out to see what was cooking. But she was only a few months old— the testy teething time—and I felt she was secure as I kneaded the bread on the counter close by.

It was a beautiful chair: sturdy, dependable, properly balanced wooden legs, with a leather back and seat. I had taken every precaution for her safety, but, yes, she did tumble right out of the chair, face down, hitting the bottom rung with her one-and-only bottom tooth, plainly visible hanging on the end of something, which had the prospects of being a root.

I don't suppose I was actually thinking that as I rushed over to the empty chair. I must have acted intuitively, without a pregnant pause, not realizing what my actions actually were, and still today I can't imagine how I could have lifted her from the floor and at the same time cupped my hand around the hanging tooth and pushed it back from whence it came.

My MD was amazed at the thought such a medical miracle could have happened, but that was so long ago, and I wish he was alive today to see the whole world smiling just to show off their own implants. You'll be surprised and thrilled to see what might happen to your life forty years from now in 2051.

Of course I'll never get the credit for cheating the fairy, who would have been there to pay a penny for it.

Chapter XXII

THE STAFF OF LIFE

*We work not only to produce
but to give value to time.*
—Delacroix

I never cease to be amazed by how the days of our lives can be tempted back for second helpings, especially lured in by the smell of home-baked bread, crusty and golden and piping hot from the oven. The day, the year, the moment breeze back to me on a ribbon held high in the hands of a young boy.

My goodness, that young boy turned sixty-six last week, and I still picture him as my rambunctious youngest child.

I remember I had been feeling somewhat delicate the day before the fair and had decided not to bake. Haydn came racing home from school with his friend Mike to find the breadboard empty and hollered, "Mom, you've just got to bake bread today. It's the fair tomorrow, and I just know your bread will win a ribbon!"

"Me?" I said. "No way! Not in competition with all the farmers' wives I know. And besides, it's an all-day process."

He harped a little more and looked so crestfallen I felt I wasn't measuring up to his expectations of a mother. So making a few quick calculations for the mixing, the three risings, the molding and baking, plus a few minutes more for keeping my youngster off the kitchen table, hoping to pop the bubbles in the dough the yeast was producing, I figured if I started right away it should hopefully be coming out of the oven before the sun was up.

The bread was perfect, the morning air had a little nip to it, and my husband was already down at the fair with the loaf of bread, exasperated when the judges said they needed a recipe in order for me to compete in the contest. I read it over the phone with my fingers crossed that he could interpret bakery language well enough to write it down. My daughter listened in on the radio for the judges' decisions, and my ten-year-old just sat there, down at the fair, mesmerizing the judges into a one-and-only decision. When the judges presented him with a ribbon for my bread, he was seen running around the aisles, holding up the ribbon shouting, "My mom's bread won this. My mom's bread!"

It was a real family affair and a very good day to remember.

To make sure that episode in our family togetherness would be remembered, I sent the story to a northwestern farm magazine, and still have the cutting from the journal, but the two dollars the staff paid me for it was spent long, long ago.

A HOLE IN ONE

The affair at the fair had given me confidence that I could rise to even greater heights with dinner and cinnamon rolls and whatever else goes into the breadbasket.

My youngest son decided I might make a hole in one if I teed off with doughnuts. He was the sports' enthusiast in the family, enjoying popularity as the junior high school football team member who could tackle two linemen in one fell swoop.

I didn't know at the time that he had an ulterior motive when he said, "Have them done by the time school is out, won't you?"

It so happened that since his football team had to practice at the high school field several blocks away, they got a good warm up running down there from the junior high school every Wednesday. And run they did, on cue, every Wednesday after until they all graduated. Out the doors of the school at the end of our block, down the street single file, up our red carpeted front steps, through the living room, through the dining room doors, into the kitchen, and without missing a beat, they swooped up a couple of man-sized frosted doughnuts from the kitchen counter with one hand and waved a salute to me with the other as they barged out the back door, across the lawn, down Yellowstone Street, across the bridge, to the field nestled along the Yellowstone River, looking up at the magnificent Absarokee Range, at a speed it usually took to beat the other guy for a touchdown.

They were a fine team, the Rangers, and all of them fine boys. On Saturday nights after the games, they would congregate, along with their girlfriends and anyone else they cared to invite, in the living room at our house, their shoes in a neat pile at the front door. The fire would be glowing already as they turned down the lights, turned up the old stereo, and danced until midnight to the melodious music of the '60s and early '70s. My husband and I chaperoned from the kitchen, making sandwiches and Kool-Aid, unless the cheerleaders decided to bake a cake, usually decorated with football posts and other things necessary for their many victories.

This weekly gathering became a sporting event carried on through football, basketball, volleyball, or any other occasion they could celebrate to have a ball, all the way through senior high school.

ROLLING WITH THE DOUGH

Plans had been made to spend Christmas at Hope's beautiful new home in Bend, Oregon, about a three-hour drive away from Corvallis. I was usually given the honor of baking dinner rolls for festive occasions, and since everyone expects them fresh and piping hot, it was decided I make them in her new kitchen, a masterpiece of architectural design and craftsmanship built by Gary, Hope's husband, with her help. So I was happy to go rolling merrily along.

Presuming a brand-new kitchen would be well stocked with everything a master chef might require for a masterpiece, I took with me only the recipe, which I knew by heart since I had created it myself.

The home was a realtor's dream: open, spacious rooms filled with daylight, hardwood floors polished to a soft-burn shine, Jacuzzi in the master bedroom, and other luxuries taken for granted nowadays. However, I had forgotten that since my daughter was employed outside the home, there was little time for cooking, and they ate out most meals. Consequently there was not much need for gadgets, such as a rolling pin, cookie cutter, or a bowl large enough to hold the dough as it starts to rise and expand beyond all expectations.

A bowl was eventually secured from the lady next door, and it took quite a while for her to find it since she had what we decided was Alzheimer's, close enough for what she called old-timers disease. She had hidden them away for safety and couldn't remember where.

A rolling pin was nowhere to be found. Neither were there any baking sheets big enough to hold the eight-dozen rolls needed to feed the crowd at Christmas dinner. So Hope ran around to the house on the other side and borrowed those necessities along with a measuring cup.

Of course when you eat out, there is simply no need to own a biscuit cutter, so I decided to make do and use a drinking glass to cut the Parker House rolls, and there was no need to go chasing after one of those.

Once started with the mixing, things went smoothly until the dough sitting in the borrowed bowl on their gas-powered stove was almost ready to be kneaded, rolled out, and cut into circles by the rim of the water-glass cookie cutter. I lifted the towel covering the very pregnant-looking dough, which was all puffed up in the manner expected, when the tea towel brushed against the lighted gas burner, which was keeping the dough at the proper temperature.

I retrieved it quickly enough so that no harm was done, except for a slightly burned towel and dim expectations for a prize-winning recipe, which surreptitiously had not rolled merrily along.

Not daunted, I rolled up my sleeves, looked around that beautiful kitchen, rolling pin in hand, and wanted to cry. Not one square inch of that meticulously grouted granite tile would yield to the whims of a rolling pin and soft, sticky dough.

I spotted a large slot underneath the countertop and asked where the cutting board might be that should occupy such a space. I could manage with that I thought, but no, they had no need yet for a cutting board. Martha Stewart herself would not have dared ask to use the beautiful dining table; it was all decked out, ready for Christmas with Martha's homemade holiday handicrafts.

Urging me along, however, was Mother's proverbial wisdom from long ago, her voice coming back to me over and again. "Necessity is the mother of invention, you know. If you can't do, you'll just have to make do, now won't you, luv?"

Oh my, yes, indeed, Mother!

I walked around disconsolate, testing the rough grout between the granite counter tiles, still shaking my head, when there, through the kitchen door leading to the utility room, just as if you, Mother, had waved your magic wand, was the most beautiful white, square, smoothly flat surface of their brand-new dryer, offering up space to be scrubbed, dried, and readied for the rolling.

Needless to say, but I will anyway, everyone said, "These are the best rolls you have ever made."

I smiled and thanked them but didn't see the sense in burdening them with explaining how they were put together. I didn't need a ribbon to show for my efforts that day.

TOAD IN THE HOLE
THE ONE THAT GOT AWAY

There was one happening in my young life, however, that would have horrified you, Mother, Father, my sisters, and the rest of the world.

Those very words, "'Twill be all right come mornin', luv," would not be forthcoming to soothe my fears because I would rather have died than tell. Instead, I shoveled the happening, with all its dirty appendages, into that cubicle of the mind called amnesia, and there it had lain dormant until it sprang to life again seventy years later, through a hole meant for a toad.

I was making your old recipe for Toad in the Hole, Mother, which you might describe as "small sausages pressed into a pan of muffin dough or pastry before baking in the oven."

I was dreaming of times gone by, when I used to make this dish for my own children, remembering how they loved *The Wind in the Willows* and the outrageous adventures of Mr. Toad of Toad Hall, their favorite character.

I smiled, about to pop a tiny toad into its bed of dough, and I was up and away, rowing down the river with Ratty and Mole, wallowing in my reverie, when out of the blue, the kitchen started moving to another address, a strange, yet familiar kitchen.

Suddenly there I was, standing at a much older table, its scratched-up legs revealing a history of little children's restless feet. Whatever distress the tabletop had suffered throughout its apparently lengthy service was covered up by a snowy white Irish linen cloth, a little frayed at the seams. The clock on the wall had stopped ticking, and my heart started beating its time.

A tiny hot sausage toad was clutched in a hand much smaller and younger than mine, and only I knew that the sausage would never reach its private hole in Mother's Toad in the Hole dish that sat in the center of that table, in the old cottage at No. 3 Gatewarth Street, Sankey Bridges, Warrington, England.

I had run home from school, knowing that Mother had made Toad that day for lunch, and I was impatiently waiting at the table for my sisters, who had lagged behind. Mother' eagle eye spotted a hole in the dough without a sausage snuggled inside, and she hastily came to the conclusion that since I was the first one at the table, I was the one who had snitched it. I winced, hearing the words disobedient, greedy, selfish, and all the other thou shall-not's we were supposed to know by heart. Remember, Mother, you made me write all ten of those commandments ten times over that night, just to make sure I knew what the rest of them were, should I decide to break another of them.

Father had walked in on the toad tirade and had turned you around to face him, speaking softly but with such authority on that day all those years ago. "Em, you are going to knock the spirit out of that girl if you keep that up. Leave her alone!"

And I wondered what I would look like without a spirit.

Even so, I was feeling anything but contrite and didn't want to go back to school. But Mother insisted with her customary, "You'll feel better once you get there," her usual remonstrance to any reason we begged to stay home. "*If* I get there," I muttered to myself. And for the first time in my young life, I disobeyed my mother and set out on an adventure that led to my keeping that nefarious tale to myself for almost the rest of my life, safely tucked away under a blanket of amnesia in a far cubicle of the mind.

As soon as I was out of earshot and eyesight, I ran for the farm at the end of our street, to the path leading around the fields to the woods, where my secret place was hidden behind the blackberry bushes.

I outran a gaggle of giggling geese trying to tell me, "Watch out! We are not as silly as they say we are, you know. We are going to get you."

I had forgotten it was Wednesday, butchering day, and when I neared the farmhouse, there was Mrs. Smith, the farmer's wife, slaughtering one of the little pigs. My heart jumped at the strange, piercing squeal and the sight of blood spurting high in the air as she slit the throat of a piglet. I ran quickly on, past the stinking midden with its sodden, steaming fodder ready to be fed to the little pigs who didn't cry that day, and I held my nose and my tears all in the same breath.

I knew where the stile was by heart, and I eagerly pulled the brambles apart, treading carefully up the steps to the top and jumping down the other side of the hedge. Grass and chickweed covered the old, worn wagon wheel ruts in the path, where cow pads had dropped long, long ago. I had never before met another soul, man nor beast, there in my secret garden.

Under a canopy of hawthorn beauty, boughs bending lovingly to send corymbs of their tiny blossoms showering confetti on my head and shoulders, I walked in beauty in veils of white, a bride walking down a cathedral aisle with a posy of daisies clutched in my hand. I was drenched in a wild perfume called hawthorn, too precious to be stoppered in any bottle.

I heard the cuckoo echoing around my world and wondered where she had laid her egg that year and who had done her mothering.

Celandine and silverweed spread their sunshine through the shadows on the grass, and I spotted the speedwell, too, blue as the sky showing now and again through my Sistine ceiling of hawthorn beauty.

I would come again, soon, to pick the first wild roses growing along the ditch, mindless of the thorns, and I would ask myself again, who on earth would have given the stately bladder campion such a sorry name and why. I would come again in winter and see the trees unfrocked yet occasionally draped in a blanket of snow.

On that spring day, my secret garden had never been so warm. So still. My real world and Mother had gone away, and I was safe.

I was sitting on the grass at the edge of the path, absorbed in picking off a daisy's petals one by one, "he loves me, he loves me not," and I neither saw nor heard them as they sneaked up on me, three of them.

They were belting each other with long, limber hawthorn branches, which they had stripped of their beautiful blossoms and were thrashing them around in a "don't give a damn" manner. I stood up to let them pass by, wondering how on earth they had found the stile. One of them was poking my arm with his stick.

"Lets play," he said, and I was too afraid to say anything before they were pushing me, lobbing me one to another, until I was rolling down the grassy bank.

One of them was shouting, "Sit on 'er, Reg. Sit on 'er."

And Reggie did, spread-eagled over my chest and looking down with an ugly sneer on his face.

As rough hands grabbed my wrists and ankles, I thought they were going to throw me in the stream, and I was afraid I would drown or die of fright and go straight to hell, praying it might be a better place than this, because I knew they were not done with their playing yet. I heard someone screaming for her mother and hoped mine would never find me there. She would say it was all my fault and that I was old enough to know better than to go around with scruff like them. She had already called me a thief that day.

I kicked and struggled, trying to keep my bloomers and my gymslip where they belonged, but my head was suddenly jerked around to one side as if it might break off, and I felt something warm and gristly, something that might have been the tough, bristled stalk of the comfrey growing along the ditch.

I know now what it must have been, that thing poking in my ear, but then it was just something that hurt and burst inside, seeping blood down my neck and into the back of my white school blouse collar. I drifted in and out of the dark, feeling as if I were clenched in the jaws of a grizzly bear intent on pounding my head into the ground until I gave up the Ghost.

By the time I stumbled to my feet, hurting and hysterical, those ruffians were racing down the path, calling me names, trampling my daisies, thrashing the hawthorn blossoms with their sticks, and heading for a stile that wasn't hidden any more.

I wanted desperately for an angel, or just anybody but them, to come along to hold me and stroke my hair, to tell me it would be all right come morning. But no one came. I knew that you would come, if only you knew, Mother, but I was so afraid of you that I knew I never would.

The inside of my head was throbbing with each deafening pain, which came with the sound and fury of waves rising and thundering to their death as they smashed against a rocky coast.

I did not want to put a dirty finger in my ear, but I did dare to pat the lobe of it with a comfrey leaf and found, to my relief, that it wasn't blood at all that dribbled from my ear, so at least I wouldn't have to explain blood-stained clothing to Mother.

I knew a lot about the flowers I gathered as a child, Mother, and when my mind sobered up again, I told myself that the sticky stuff I was wiping off my neck must have been sap from the comfrey stalk. I kept on wiping my arms, my legs, but when I reached down to my knees a sickly feeling went shivering through me. My bloomers—they weren't there! What would you have done, Mother, if they weren't in the wash that week?

I labored up the hill, stifling my sobs, but cried out in relief as I reached the top. Those boys had taken off with my bloomers, and there they were, hanging on a branch on the far side of the lane.

I sat on the turnstile at the railway crossing for a while, watching for the school children to come along so that I could run home ahead of my sisters and hide somewhere.

The next day Mother looked out to see Reggie in our backyard, his hands in a stranglehold around my neck. She was outside the gate before he knew what hit him, the stiff-bristled broom flaying the air and landing with a whack across his bottom. All the while, she screamed at me, "What on earth did you do to make him choke you like that? He almost did you in!"

You asked me that question many times, Mother, and I always told you "Nothing," which was the truth, and when you stopped asking, I must have stopped remembering until I had left home and had a family of my own and one day decided to make Toad in the Hole.

I never went back to my hawthorn lane, as far as I can remember, and wonder now how such a thing could ever have happened in that beautiful garden of Paradise, where the secret has stayed hidden for more than eighty years. I wish with all of my heart that I had the courage and good sense enough to have run home to hear you say those comforting words to take my fears away, Mother.

You don't remember them any more you say?

Well, I still say them to myself once in a while now that you are gone and I am old enough to have learned many lessons, including this one, Mother: "'Twill be all right come mornin', luv."

I have sometimes prayed for those boys of dirty hands and dirtier thoughts.

And now, here they all stand, naked before me, begging forgiveness in their old age.

But it is impossible to forgive without forgetting, isn't it? I did not ask for second helpings of this no-good, indigestible day in my childhood, so I might just as well chuck it in the stinking midden and let it go. The pigs will know what to do with it!

And once again I will only remember being safe, there in the past. Yet there is no way to rebury that part of my life, and I am forced to acknowledge the incident and its impact upon my life during all those years in between. The forgetting years, when I kept that dark secret bottled up tight until it fermented and finally blew its cork.

What role has that buried incident played in the sequence of my life's unfolding? What happened to my psyche in those moments frozen in fear?

Did my mind, my mentality, my soul become all twisted up in a psyche knot pinned up with my mother's black hair?

Will all this introspection now reveal that I am back there still, a child going on ninety-two?

I do hope you are not worrying about me, Mother, since I still live in my little grey home in the West taking care of myself and my home, and yes, Father, I still would rather write than eat and shall until the day I reach one hundred years or die trying because I belong to the family of Hope and know with all my heart that hope has nothing to do with fear or malice.

CHAPTER XXIII

COMING TO CONCLUSIONS

Samuel Butler was known to say, "Life is the art of drawing sufficient conclusions from insufficient premises."

Regardless of unforeseen circumstance between times, as far back as I remember into longevity, I like to always have something, anything, planned ahead for which I may *hope* to realize.

Many times, it's something as simple as looking forward to a dinner and movie date with my young old friends. Or hoping my grandson will show up to fix my computer, or to see a movie more appealing than the appalling *Knocked Up*.

I enjoyed the time I spent waiting to see and hear *The King's Speech*, for example, even though seventy-two years ago I listened live, on the wireless, tears in my eyes, as did millions of other Brits, to a failed speech from a royal who was born to be a leader.

It's the little things that mean a lot in later life, and you have the time to enjoy them to your heart's content. But like me, if you are or have been victim to the fear of falling or some other malady, you must go through the scene in your mind, crossing each bridge as you approach it to assure yourself that you are going to cross it rather than falling into the Willamette River with your eyes wide open. Banish your fears and you will be proud of your prowess.

It took many years for me to really understand the true meaning of the word spirit as it could be applied to my life.

We can all feel some kind of spirit (the breath of life) urging us on in all aspects of our existence on earth as nations try to communicate. And I ask, (with my bottle corked and sitting on the shelf), "Why on earth, then, is this gift of spirit wasted in the propagation of everlasting war rather than living in the infinite joy of peace."

I am not a scholar of religion, but St. Paul's writings reveal these words to us. And I think, "What this?"

The words sound boastful, but as I read between them, the apostle is speaking of spirit—the breath of life—and his desire to share experiential knowledge of the kindred spirit and the glory of it. His spirit, he is saying, is there to be shared and used up in the cause of all men. And women!

At the closing of this book, Mother, I wish to share a little wisdom from Socrates. When he was asked which came first, the chicken or the egg, that wise man replied, "The chicken, of course. The egg is just a possibility." So in my younger days, naturally, I never did count my chickens before they were hatched; I would never know what to do with them all. And nowadays I would much prefer to count the eggs fresh from the grocery shelf and buy just as many of them as I need.

When I was a child, there was a party game, the prize going to the youngster with the best answer to the question, "Why did the chicken cross the road?"

It was fun and much more stimulating to use the head rather than wearing out the thumbs for nothing in particular.

All I care about chickens today is that those who raise them commercially will have the heart to treat them more humanely than I see on TV. Overcrowding, falling over one another, squawking in chorus at their lack of pecking room, let alone their longing to ruffle their feathers with some dignity.

And like all humanity, if they have a stomach, surely they should have a sacrificial meal before they are beheaded.

But now, at my age I don't give a peck about chickens crossing roads. All I care about is that they aren't run over.

I'd try it myself if there was a handsome young man over there who knows how to cook one.

So be prepared and stand each burden calmly. Whatever will be, will be.

Never look back with regret on whatever you did in good faith, and no matter what the consequence, you can sing along with Doris Day.

Que sera, sera.
Whatever will be, will be!
The future's not ours to see,

Que sera, sera.

Be a creature of habit so the small stuff is well rehearsed and performed mechanically when you are swamped with more important demands on your time and responsibilities. A wise person once said, "Life should not be remembered by the number of breaths we take," Mother, "but by the moments that take our breath away."

It is morning, dear Mother, and everything is still all right with me no matter what the weather or whatever.

Just one last thank you for the way you raised me, Mother.

You gave me courage in the face of adversity. You gave me hope when despair was knocking at our door.

You made me see reality through the rose-colored glasses I was tempted to wear.

You gave me room to see the world as it is and not as I think it should be. To rise with the dawn knowing your words can ring true if I make then so and revel in them.

'Twill be all right come mornin', luv.

For evermore.

Photos

Granny Knight, riding in a Charabanc
1930, Warrington England

Unilever Drama Festival

Unilever Drama Festival

The Wedding
September 11th, 1943, Warrington England

Coming to America on the Mauratania 1945

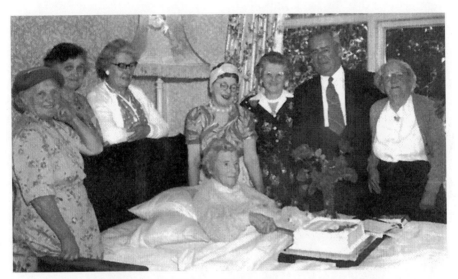

May 26, 1960, Granny Hope on her 100th birthday

The tablecloth

The tablecloth, detail

Picnic with Ray
2001 Corvallis, OR

Irene, covered in stickers, and her first grandson
2011, Corvallis, OR

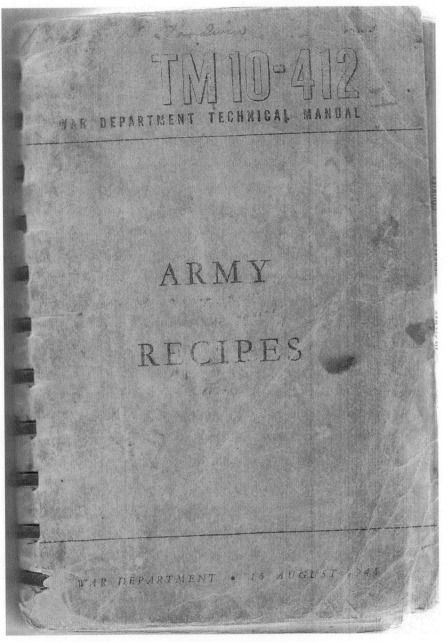

Army Recipes Cookbook

Bird's Eye Cookbook

White House Cook Book

18162744R00109

Made in the USA
Lexington, KY
18 October 2012